SELL, KEEP, OR TOSS?

How to Downsize a Home, Settle an Estate, and Appraise Personal Property

D0055121

HARRY L. RINKER

SELL, KEEP, OR TOSS?

How to Downsize a Home, Settle an Estate, and Appraise Personal Property

HOUSE OF COLLECTIBLES

New York
Toronto
London
Sydney
Auckland

HARRY L. RINKER

**HOUSE OF
COLLECTIBLES**

Visit the House of Collectibles Web site: *www.houseofcollectibles.com*

Text design by Nora Rosansky

Library of Congress Cataloging-in-Publication Data
Rinker, Harry L., 1966–
  Sell, keep, or toss? : what to do with a lifetime of treasures / Harry L. Rinker.
    p. cm.
  Includes index.
  ISBN-13: 978-0-375-72240-0 (trade pbk. : alk. paper) 1. Older people—Finance, Personal. 2. Valuation. 3. Personal property. 4. House furnishings. 5. Collectibles. 6. Heirlooms. 7. Estate planning. I. Title.
  HG179.R53 2007
  332.0240084'6—dc22

                                                            2007010654

10 9 8 7 6 5 4 3 2 1

Printed in the United States of America

First Edition

Contents

Acknowledgments

I write all my books in my head, a process that often takes years, before committing my final thoughts on paper. As a result, I find myself hard-pressed to identify all the individuals who commented upon ideas I bounced off them or offered their original thoughts to questions I posed. The only way to include everyone in this acknowledgment is to offer a general thanks for their involvement.

A few special thanks are in order. This is the first book I have written since marrying Dr. Linda K. Rinker. A nurse by training and an academic administrator by profession, she is quite familiar with the birthing process. When I finally finished the manuscript, she exclaimed, "I have never witnessed anything like this." Alas, for her, I am planning to write several other books.

Dana Morykan, friend and associate, has worked with me for over fifteen years. She did the initial editing of this manuscript. She also offered many helpful comments, all of which strengthened the presentation.

Authors have visions. Editors turn them into reality. Special thanks to Rahel Lerner, editor for antiques and collectibles titles, for having faith in this project and seeing it through its manuscript, copyediting, and proofing stages. Helena Santini directed the editorial efforts during the final publishing stages. Thanks also to Patricia Dublin, associate managing editor, Carolyn Roth, production editor, Lisa Montebello, production manager, and Nora Rosansky, designer, for their contributions.

Finally, thanks to you, the readers and users of this book. I would very much like to hear from you what you found helpful, what you did not, and what you wish might have been included but was not. E-mail me at harrylrinker@aol.com or write me at 5093 Vera Cruz Road, Emmaus, PA 18049.

Harry L. Rinker
Vera Cruz, PA
September 2007

Introduction

It all started with a telephone call.

A gentleman who was serving as the executor of his aunt's estate called to inquire about an estate appraisal. I explained that I could list between twenty and twenty-five objects an hour when doing a written appraisal; a full house required two to three days on-site and about equal time researching and writing the report. I ended by quoting my hourly and day rates. When I finished, there was a prolonged period of silence.

"Are you there," I asked.

"Yes," he replied softly. I knew immediately that the projected appraisal cost shocked him. After another short period of hesitation, he responded, "All I really want to know is if there is anything worthwhile in my aunt's house. I do not want to throw out anything valuable. Could I buy an hour or two of your time and have you walk through the house and just take a look around?"

It was a reasonable request. This gentleman did not need an appraisal. He needed advice. He was overwhelmed by the task of disposing of the furnishings and other items in his aunt's house. He had never served as an executor of an estate before. I had never done a walk-through appraisal. New experiences are fun.

I spent a little over an hour walking through the house commenting on the value of things that I saw and asking many questions about things I expected to see but did not. The gentleman made notes. I took notes about two pieces so I could do additional research when I returned to my office.

When I finished, he asked if I was willing to sit down and explain the options he had in disposing of the items I had just seen. Again, I agreed.

This was the first of hundreds of such walk-through appraisals I have done since that date. Each has been a challenge. In almost every instance, I pointed out things the person would have discarded whose sale more than paid for my visit. In those rare instances where I did not, the client's peace of mind in knowing that he was not disposing of anything valuable was worth the cost of the walk-through.

Thanks to the demands of these walk-through appraisals, I have become one of the last generalists in the antiques and collectibles field. I know a little something about every collecting category and I have developed a keen sense of what I know and when I need to make notes and do more research.

Knowledge in the antiques and collectibles field is cumulative. The more objects you handle, the more you learn. Thanks to these walk-through appraisals, I have learned a great deal.

My expertise in doing walk-through appraisals was one of the reasons I was chosen to be the Collector Inspector on Home & Garden Television (HGTV). Seventy-eight episodes of *The Collector Inspector* aired between October 2, 2002, and December 2004. The desire to share my walk-through appraisal experiences with a wider public was the genesis for this book. The advice it contains is the advice I give my clients. You will find the advice solid and down-to-earth.

In addition, I drew upon my personal experiences in settling my parents' estates, as well as the estates of several of my family members and friends. Learn from your mistakes is an old cliché. Again, I learned a great deal.

Finally, I am a collector. My collection contains over fifty thousand objects. I needed to write this book for my wife, my extended family, and, perhaps most importantly, for me.

The Evolution of the Book

When I first conceived this book, I saw its focus limited to the questions involved in settling an estate. "Dead People's Stuff: Dealing With the Stuff Your Parents Left Behind When They Died" was my working title. By the time I circulated the proposal of the book, its proposed title had been amended to "What Am I Going to Do?: How to Dispose of Your Parents,' Relatives,' or Friends' Possessions." Ms. Rahel Lerner at Random House argued strenuously and finally convinced me that the subject matter applied as much to a person or couple who had to downsize as it did to an executor of an a estate faced with disposing of personal property. Hence, the information presented in this book applies to both situations.

The book is divided into five parts. Chapter one deals with how secondary market value is determined. Its application is much broader than this book.

Chapters two and three cover basic and thorny issues that need to be addressed before the actual process of selling, keeping, and/or tossing begins.

Chapters four through six focus first on how to divide objects into sell, keep, and toss piles, how to dispose of a collection, and the delicate issue of dealing with family and friends. The chapters' secondary theme is how to separate what you want to keep for yourself or others from those things you want to sell.

Chapters seven through thirteen describe in detail the venues available for the disposal of objects, including a chapter on donations. The pluses and minuses of each sale method are evaluated.

Chapter thirteen is about tossing things. Hopefully, if I have served you well, you will discover that you have to toss very little and can even earn some money performing that task.

Chapter fourteen is a bonus, written for those individuals whose life choices have made it necessary for me to write *Sell, Keep, or Toss?* Those readers who are open to changing their approach to the disposal of their things prior to their demise are encouraged to read it. Those who are not can avoid it.

A Word or Two of Warning

I love adages, clichés, and truisms. This book is loaded with them. This is no lie. I also like puns. If you read carefully, you will find them scattered throughout the book as well. I write in my own vernacular style. It is who I am.

I also have a reputation for being opinionated. After reading this book, you will understand why. I am not apologizing for this either. I enjoy my reputation for telling it as I see it.

My Opinions and Only My Opinions

This book is a blend of the objective and subjective. It is filled with fact. It is also filled with my opinions. You should have no difficulty telling one from the other.

The most important thing to understand is that there is no one right answer for the disposal of personal property. There are dozens of possibilities. My role as author is to familiarize you with these possibilities. Your responsibility is to decide which options are right for you. The right answer for you is the one you select. Never forget this as you read this book.

Was This Book Helpful?

I expect this book to remain in print for many years. I do plan to revise it from time to time. Hence, I need your help.

Did you find my advice helpful? What worked and did not work? What did you do that was successful and does not appear in this book?

Finally, I welcome learning about your personal experiences in downsizing and settling the personal property of an estate. We can learn from each other.

E-mail your account to me at harrylrinker@aol.com or write Sell, Keep, or Toss?, 5093 Vera Cruz Road, Emmaus, PA 18049.

Harry L. Rinker
Vera Cruz, PA / Brookfield, CT
November 2006

CHAPTER ONE

What Are My Things Worth?

THERE are no fixed values in the secondary resale market for antiques, collectibles, and used goods. Value floats. It is momentary, influenced by a host of variables such as time, place, and circumstance. In the end, value is what an object brings at the moment you sell it. Your challenge is to maximize this value. *Sell, Keep, or Toss?* shows you how.

Defining Terms

Just as in sports where you cannot tell the players without a scorecard, you cannot understand the terms used in this book unless we are on the same page.

ANTIQUE—an object made before 1963.

Although this is not the standard definition of the term, when thinking about selling household goods it is helpful to consider all products made before 1963 as antiques. Do you remember where you were when you heard that President Kennedy had been assassinated? Then, sad to say, you are an antique in today's marketplace, and so are most of your household goods.

COLLECTIBLE—an object made between 1963 and 1980.

Chances are these are the objects from your children's rather than your generation. Memorabilia from the beatnik, hippie, and psychedelic eras is hot. The same applies to post-World War II modernist furniture. Objects from this more recent period can fetch surprisingly high prices.

Antiques and collectibles have a stable secondary retail market. You can research values and trust them.

DESIRABLE—an object made between 1980 and the present.

I use the term "desirable" because I want a neutral term to describe this contemporary material. What differentiates antiques and collectibles from desirables is that the secondary market for desirables is speculative. Value is in a constant state of flux: for example, Beanie Babies.

REUSABLE—an antique, collectible, or desirable whose primary value is reuse.

The vast majority of the objects you will be dealing with fall into this category. Many household objects, especially from before 1980, were built to perform for many years of use, and their value to buyers is in that continued usefulness.

Further complicating the picture is the fact that there is not one value, but many. In some cases, a specific value governs the worth of an object. In other cases, a single object can have multiple values. Confused? Do not be. Understanding value is not as complicated as it first appears.

When evaluating objects you are thinking of selling, keeping, or tossing, begin by considering three basic values: (1) collector value, (2) decorative value, and (3) reuse value. You need to master these three values first before you factor in other value considerations that will allow you to more precisely determine the true secondary market resale value of your things.

Collector Value

Collector value is the amount a collector will pay for an object. However, it is based on three key assumptions. First, the collector does not already have an example of the object in his collection. Second, he wants the object. Third, the object is priced at a point he is willing to pay.

Collectors pay a premium price only for the first example of an object they buy. Collectors may buy duplicates, but never at the same price as the first example. If they are going to be tempted to buy a second example, it has to be priced at twenty to twenty-five percent of what they paid for the first example.

Most collectors own one or more examples of the commonly found and even hard-to-find objects in their collecting category. When they go to an auction, show, or sale, they are seeking scarce items. Chances are better than ninety-five percent that a collector already owns an example of the object you are trying to sell.

TIP I want you to make the assumption that every object you are thinking of selling, keeping, or tossing is common. The biggest mistake people make when attempting to determine the worth of their objects is assuming they are scarcer than they are.

When buying from a private individual, collectors expect to buy at a discount. Collectors pay top dollar only when buying from a dealer at an antiques show or bidding against a rival collector at an auction. The amount of discount collectors expect to pay depends on the scarcity of the object. If the object is common, the expected discount can be as high as seventy-five percent of the secondary market retail price. Even then, a collector may not be tempted if he owns multiple examples already. If the object is scarce, collectors still expect a twenty-five- to thirty-percent discount.

Historically collector value was the primary value used to price all antiques and collectibles. This is no longer true in the twenty-first century where collector value applies only to the scarce, high-end pieces in any collecting category. The number of such pieces is limited, often fewer than fifty. Value for the rest of the objects has to be found elsewhere.

Decorative Value

Decorative value is the dominant secondary market resale value in the twenty-first century. More antiques and collectibles are sold for decorative purposes than are sold to collectors. My best guess is that this figure exceeds seventy percent of all goods sold.

Thanks to decorating gurus such as Martha Stewart and a host of cable television shows, antiques and collectibles now play an integral role in our lifestyle. Every decorating style from shabby chic to country to modernism incorporates antiques and collectibles into their decorating scheme. It is all about achieving The Look!

Decorative value is multifaceted. The high side of decorative value is *pizzazz value*. An object with pizzazz value has the ability to attract the immediate focus of anyone entering a room in which it is displayed. A pizzazz object usually is large and bold in color and nature. It dominates. Ideally it has aesthetic appeal as well, but more important is that it captures everyone's attention. It has to have universal, not personal appeal. Pizzazz objects generally are assigned a high secondary market resale value.

Conversation value is closely related to pizzazz value. Often smaller and more personal in nature, objects with conversation value invoke discussion and questions when encountered. Questions can range from What is this? to What is the story behind this? Conversation objects are more intimate than pizzazz objects. Pizzazz objects create a general buzz while conversational objects encourage one-on-one or small group conversation.

Nostalgia value is a decorative value, although some will argue it is strong enough to stand alone. An object has nostalgia value when it evokes family and/or childhood memories in the mind of its owner—a piece fondly remembered from visits to the grandparents or a favorite childhood book or toy. Objects with nostalgia value always are displayed. Owners want to bask in their memory daily. They also want to share their memory with others.

Decorative value is in a constant state of flux. Styles are continuously changing.

TIP A quick way to determine the current hot decorating styles is to visit a major bookstore and quickly thumb through the decorating periodicals. Make certain you check all styles, not just look at those you like. What you see is what buyers want. What you do not see is out.

Change occurs continually within a decorating style. Country is an excellent example. The country decorating pendulum swings between the rough primitive weathered look at one end and a highly romanticized vision of the successful farmer and small businessman on the other. The popularity of animals—cows are in, cows are out; roosters are in, roosters are out—changes every few years. This also applies to colors and decorative themes, for example, watermelons versus strawberries.

The result is a twenty-first-century antiques and collectibles secondary resale market that is trendy. Decorating trends last from a few years to a few months. One thing is certain—none last forever.

The desire for change inherent in the decorating market has impacted the collecting community. Throughout much of the twentieth century, collectors assumed the value of their antiques and collectibles would continually increase over time. They received a rude awakening in the 1990s when the antiques and collectibles market also became subject to trends. The era of the blue-chip antiques and collectibles is over. Collecting categories such as early American pattern glass, cast iron toys, and Model T Fords, once the darlings of the collecting community, are in decline. A future renaissance is highly unlikely.

FACT When looking at objects you are thinking of selling, keeping, or tossing always ask first how do they relate to the current hot collecting and decorating trends?

Reuse Value

The vast majority of the objects you are considering selling, keeping, or tossing will have reuse value rather than collector or decorative value. Reuse value and recyclable value are identical. An object has reuse value when its primary value rests in the possibility of the object's continued use for the purpose for which it was originally intended.

I am a Pennsylvania German. As such, I was exposed to the philosophy of "it is too good to throw out" and "I will never know when I might need it." As a result, every attic, closet, basement, garage, and shed in Pennsylvania German country is filled with dozens, if not hundreds, of objects that still have reuse value. Based on my travels, I know this philosophy is not unique to the Pennsylvania Germans.

When I established my first apartment, I furnished it with hand-me-downs from my aunts and uncles and other extended family members. I was advised to find other things I needed at auction, thrift shops, and even antiques shops where things were cheaper than new. Also implied, but not stated, was the theory that older objects were better made and of higher quality.

Cheaper than new is the key to selling objects for reuse value. The antiques and collectibles trade is loaded with objects that are cheaper than new. Dinnerware, clothing and accessories, flatware, furniture, jewelry, musical instruments, stemware, and textiles such as table linens are just the tip of the iceberg. Cheaper than new means that the antiques and collectibles are selling at one-quarter to one-third the price of a similar object purchased new. What makes these objects so attractive besides the price? The answer is far more variety than the standard selection in a department or chain store.

Reuse value is the primary value that applies to the household goods, for example, pots and pans, clothing, etc., you use on an everyday basis. The first inclination when encountering this material is to box and toss anything you do not want or consider useful. Do not do this. Just because the objects may no longer have value to you does not mean someone else will not want them.

FACT Value is in the eye of the beholder. Just because an object has no value to you does not mean it does not have value to someone else.

Reuse value when applied to household goods ranges between five and ten cents on the initial purchase dollar. Again, avoid the temptation of looking at these numbers and deciding not to bother. In a worst-case scenario, you may only recover one or two hundred dollars, but to my mind, one hundred dollars is far better than no hundred dollars.

Family Value

Family value is primarily an emotional and sentimental value. It also can be a monetary value, although most of the time it is not. Is family value the most important value? In respect to you, it most certainly is. In respect to anyone else, it has no impact whatsoever.

Family value prevents you from objectively seeing the actual secondary retail market value of your objects. The more difficult it is for you to part with an object, the higher the value you tend to assign to it. In reality you do not want to part with it. Even if someone is willing to pay the price you ask, the act of selling is painful.

♦ TIP If you cannot bear to part with a family object, do not. These are the first items that belong on your keep pile.

Family value is highly personal. It does not automatically transfer from one generation to another. Your fond memories of great-grandmother's vase may not be those of your children.

The following telephone conversation has taken place so often that I have completely lost track of the number of times:

> "My husband and I are downsizing and the children do
>   not want my grandparents' china service."
> "When was the last time you used it?"
> "We never use it."
> "Why not?"
> "It is too valuable to use."
> "No wonder the children do not want it."

♦ FACT Creating memories is the key to successfully passing a family heirloom to the next generation.

Today's young adults do not want things they cannot use. If you want your family treasures to be treasured by the next generation, you need to create memories with them. Use your grandparents' dinnerware, flatware, and stemware when entertaining your children. Memories are made standing around the kitchen sink washing these items by hand and talking. Serve your grandchild hot chocolate from grandmother's chocolate set. Let your grandson play with your grandfather's Buddy L truck. Share your family jewelry with your daughter and daughter-in-law. Take pictures while you do all this and pass these down with the objects.

Most importantly, write down and record the family stories associated with your family heirlooms. You probably played "whisper down the alley" or "telephone" as a child. Remember how distorted the initial phrase was when it reached the end of the line? The same holds true for family stories passed down orally.

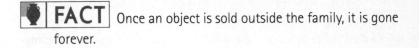 **FACT** Once an object is sold outside the family, it is gone forever.

I bought a grandfather clock at auction. When the sale was over, a family member came to me and said, "You now own our family's clock." "No, I do not," I replied, "I own my family clock."

There are no subtleties here. If you want family objects to stay in the family, you have to work at it. If you make the decision to sell family objects, you need to put your emotions and sentiments aside and make a cold, objective assessment of their worth. If you cannot, you need to hire someone who can.

Book Value

Visit any major bookstore and you will find hundreds of antiques and collectibles price guides ranging from general guides covering the entire antiques and collectibles market to guides focusing on a single collecting category. You can spend a small fortune and a great deal of time using them to determine the value of the objects you are considering selling, keeping, or tossing. If you do not understand how to use them, you will obtain far more invalid than valid information.

Price guides are exactly what their name implies. The prices in them are designed to serve as a guide. The prices are not absolute, in fact, far from it. When using any price guide, read the introduction. Most explicitly state what the values listed mean.

FACT Book value is retail value—a buyer's value, not a seller's value.

Book or price guide value reflects the value someone should expect to pay for an antique or collectible when purchasing it at an antiques mall or show. It reflects the maximum/full secondary market retail value. Book value is synonymous with collector value when the collector is buying in the traditional marketplace.

I have edited or authored more than forty price guides. Every one contained the following: "This book is not a seller's guide. Do not be mistaken and assume it is. If you have an object listed in this book and wish to sell it, expect to receive 30% to 40% of the price listed if the object is commonly found and 50% to 60% if the object is hard to find." To be honest, these percentages are generous. Any price guide I edit in the future will have these percentages cut in half. The changing nature of the twenty-first-century secondary retail market requires this.

FACT Antiques and collectibles are bought at retail and sold at wholesale.

Price guides assume the user can properly identify the object he is researching, but often users make mistakes. When this occurs, the price information is invalid. Once a person has a fixed price in his mind in respect to the value of an object, it is extremely hard to change it. It is important to remain flexible on the pricing of items you are trying to sell. If you initially thought an item had a resale value of $75, and it turns out only to have a resale value of $25, you will be disappointed, but remember that this is still money in your pocket.

Everyone who sells an object wants to achieve book value and, more often than not, expects to achieve it. But as I've explained, book value is the price that a dealer or auction house will get for the item—selling it on your own you are unlikely to get that price, but what you get can still be worthwhile.

The vast majority of antiques and collectibles price guides, especially the guides focusing on a single collecting category, are written by collectors and dealers who may have a vested interest in propping up the market. Prices often reflect what dealers hope to achieve when selling to a customer or serve to justify the prices they have charged in the past. A few individuals have deliberately used price guides to manipulate secondary retail prices upward.

Book Price Versus Sale Percentage Expectations

There is a direct correlation between book price and the amount you should expect to receive when you offer an object for sale privately. These percentages are not absolute, only a guide.

BOOK VALUE	SALE PERCENTAGE EXPECTATIONS
Under $25	10%
$26 to $250	15% to 20%
$251 to $1,000	25%
$1,001 to $2,500	35%
$2,501 to $10,000	40%
Over $10,001	50%

These percentages are low. It pays to think conservatively. Better to be surprised than disappointed.

The more effort you expend, the more likely you will exceed these percentages, especially for objects that book over $1,000.

Not all price guide prices are questionable. Many price guides provide an honest reflection of the secondary retail market. How do you determine which is which? The answer is to field test the prices. Are the prices in the book the same as those you see at antiques malls or shows? Remember, many antiques and collectibles are sold at discounts ranging from ten to twenty percent or more. As a result, price guide prices should be near and certainly not significantly above field prices.

Once you understand secondary market retail prices, you are in a better position to understand the prices you can expect to receive when selling your items.

You can also check if the prices in the price guide reflect those found on the Internet, especially at eBay. More and more price guides, especially the general guides, are using Internet values. If you see a disparity of greater than twenty-five percent between the price guide values and those found on the Internet, you need to be concerned. Checking online can help you identify a percentage by which you can cut the price guide values to obtain an accurate reflection of the true secondary retail market value.

One final note: Book value only applies to antiques and collectibles. Alas, there is no book to which you can turn to find the secondary retail market value for common household goods, the majority of those items whose value is reuse. These values can best be determined by observing the prices for which these objects sell at local auctions, tag sales, and garage sales.

Internet Value

While the Internet is far bigger than eBay, prices realized on eBay are rapidly becoming a standard measure of what an object is worth. In many collecting categories, including depression glass and collector edition items, the news is not good. In others, such as postcards, it is terrific.

TIP When determining the value of an object sold on the Internet, do not forget to add the shipping and handling costs.

Internet auctions often allow you to examine the bidding pattern and show the number of bids. When looking at the bidding pattern, focus on the amount bid by the third bidder. No matter the price at which the object closed, the third bid is a better reflection of the object's worth than the winning bid.

The principle is simple. Once the top bidder is removed from the picture and a second identical object appears for sale, the second bidder only has to make one bid above what the third bidder is willing to pay. It takes the sale of several dozen examples of the same object on the Internet to establish a stable secondary retail market value that can be trusted.

FACT Almost everything you are considering keeping, selling, or tossing is mass-produced. If there is one, there is another. In fact, if there is one, there are probably hundreds or thousands more.

The number of bids is not the same as the number of bidders. Individuals often bid several times. Therefore, when checking the bid pattern of an object sold on the Internet, take note of the actual number of bidders. A small number of bidders indicate a limited amount of interest. Most eBay auctions have fewer than a dozen bidders, many have under five.

The antiques and collectibles community is in the middle of a major debate about price validity. Traditional dealers and collectors continue to discount the importance of Internet prices. Others argue they are a true indication of market worth.

The truth falls somewhere in between. The value of commonly found, above average, and even some hard-to-find items on the Internet generally falls below book value. High-end values are established by catalog auction and antiques show prices. However, when these items appear on the Internet, they sometimes sell significantly above these prices.

Factors That Influence Value

The values discussed thus far—collector, decorative, reuse, family, book, and Internet—are types of values. All are subject to a wide range of factors that influence the final numerical value. Understanding these influences will assist you in deciding what to sell, keep, or toss.

Condition, Scarcity, and Desirability are the Big Three value considerations. All other value considerations are secondary. All value considerations apply across the board, whether the object is antique, collectible, desirable, or reusable.

Condition

Condition, condition, condition! Condition is the key to value. Condition dominated value considerations throughout most of the twentieth century and the first few years of the twenty-first century. In fact, condition became and remains an obsession with young collectors. Young collectors want everything to look like it was made yesterday.

Historically condition grades were limited to poor, fair, good, very good, and excellent. Grading was subjective and not emphasized heavily. Today the condition grades have expanded more than twofold to include: salvageable for parts, poor but restorable, fair, good, very good, fine, very fine, excellent, near mint, and mint. Grading is now much more defined, albeit still subjective.

FACT Most antiques and collectibles are graded on a scale of one to ten with ten the highest possible grade. Investment grade objects must be in very fine or better condition if made before 1960 and in near mint or better condition if made after that date.

The grading craze began in the toy community in the late 1980s when the concept of MIB (mint in the box) was created. An MIB toy showed virtually no signs of play and was housed in its period box, also in very fine or better condition. The concept reached the extreme with NRFB (never removed from the box). NRFB described an object whose packaging was never opened. The craze for MIB and NRFB has thankfully faded away.

The arm's-length test is the key to grading today. Hold an object at arm's length. If you see any visible damage, no matter how slight, the value is impacted, often quite heavily. Arm's length is the distance you stand from a wall or shelf to view objects.

TIP When you think you have an object graded properly, lower its grade by one or two levels. Sellers often overgrade objects in the hope of obtaining the highest value.

Historically, damage was assessed as major and minor. A small chip or nick in a nineteenth-century American historical view Staffordshire plate might result in a ten- to twenty-percent price reduction. A major defect would reduce the price fifty to sixty percent. Today any damage, no matter how minor, to the visible surface reduces the value by fifty percent or more. Major damage makes a piece virtually nonsalable.

In respect to nonvisible surfaces, the following applies: The more common the object, the less tolerance of damage. The simple truth is that the survival rate for objects is far higher than anyone ever imagined. EBay proved this. As a result, buyers have rapidly learned to be patient and wait until an object arrives on the market in the condition they demand rather than buy a lesser condition object and trade up later.

In modern objects bought primarily for reuse, only those in excellent or better condition sell. If a modern object is damaged in any way, it is best to toss it.

The days of the fix-it-upper are gone. Today's buyers want objects that are room ready, that is, objects that can be taken directly from the sale venue to the new owner's home and used, either functionally or for display.

Typically less than twenty-five percent of the antiques and collectibles you own or find in an estate will be of sufficient condition grade to interest a collector. Do not lose hope. Individuals buying for decorative value are more tolerant of condition flaws. There are other avenues, discussed in later chapters, that are open to you through which you can recover money for objects your first inclination is to toss.

Scarcity

The Internet, especially eBay, redefined scarcity. America's homes are still loaded with goods. Assuming that everything already is in the hands of collectors, dealers, and museums is a false assumption. The survival rate of objects is ten times higher than anyone imagined. I had an inkling this was true based on what I saw over the past ten years at appraisal clinics and the homes that I visited as Home & Garden Television's Collector Inspector, and the Internet has confirmed it.

When someone tells me they have never seen an example of an object before, my stock response is: "Where did you look?" Even if you are actively engaged in the selling of antiques, collectibles, and desirables, do not fall into the trap of assuming an object is scarcer than it is. As stated earlier, assume every object is common.

TIP Do not even think of using the term "rare." Nothing is rare anymore. Rare is one of the most abused terms on the Internet.

Determine scarcity on a four-point scale with one assigned to common objects, two to relatively easy to find objects, three to hard to find objects, and four to scarce objects.

COMMON objects are those you can find in a matter of hours or a few days if you want an example. Examples are always for sale whenever you do an eBay search. Examples are frequently found in very fine or better condition.

EASY TO FIND means the search will require a few weeks rather than a few days to find an example in the condition and price one is willing to pay.

HARD TO FIND objects are those found several times a year. Only one or two is in acceptable condition. It is at this level that scarcity begins to affect value.

SCARCE objects come on the market only every few years. Collectors and museums own most examples. However, again thanks to the Internet, examples do appear.

Desirability

Condition and scarcity are important. But what happens when you have a scarce one hundred-year-old object in excellent condition and no buyer? The answer is simple: The object has no value.

FACT An object has no value without a buyer.

The existence of a buyer is the critical component of value in the twenty-first century. Historically buyers sought out the objects. Traditional buyers love the hunt. Stories about the hunt add to the mystique associated with owning an object.

Today buyers focus more on buying than hunting. They will hunt when necessary, but much prefer when objects are brought to them. This is why selling via the Internet, whether directly, through Internet auction, or Internet bidding at a live auction, continues to gain popularity.

There is a direct link between desirability and existing collecting and decorating trends. When a collecting category, decorator style, or personality are hot, objects associated with it jump in value. When interest cools, values fall.

♦ | TIP The best time to sell is when a market runs hot. Once it peaks, get out fast. Values plummet.

Desirability is not evenly distributed geographically. Although the antiques and collectibles market of the twenty-first century is global, local, regional, and national value remains an important pricing consideration.

When considering the potential sale of an object, the "where will it bring the best price" question must be asked. If you want to maximize the value of the items you want to sell, you need to sell them in the best market possible. A one-market approach to selling items often reduces the potential secondary market sales value of the object.

♦ | FACT There are a limited number of collectors for every object.

Desirability also is affected by supply and demand. There is not an endless supply of collectors, just as there is not an endless number of reuse buyers. Once demand is satisfied, value drops. A collecting category comprising thousands of collectors is the exception, not the rule. Many collecting categories have fewer than five hundred members. While closet collectors, those unknown to the collecting community, play a role, their numbers are limited as well.

The United States Postal Service sold over seven million Elvis Presley stamps to collectors. Most were saved. Are there seven million Elvis Presley collectors out there? No way! Are there seven million stamp collectors who want the Elvis Presley stamp out there? No way! The Elvis stamp is a glut on the market.

Old/Age

Old is no longer a value consideration. In the nineteenth and first half of the twentieth century age was a value. The fact that a hundred-year-old object survived was enough to make it valuable in collectors' eyes.

FACT Revering an object simply because it is old clouds your ability to judge its value.

Age is a state of mind. The objects with which one grew up and associated as a young adult remain forever young in one's mind. There is no way they can be old as I remember them. What a sixty-five-year-old remembers is very different from what a thirty-five-year-old remembers. The 1950s are ancient to someone born after 1976. But to these younger collectors, the mere fact that an object has endured over time is not sufficient to make it valuable.

Period Box

What constitutes a complete unit? Is the object and box in which it came sufficient? The answer is no. A complete unit consists of the object, the box, the packaging, and all support literature.

TIP Before you throw out any box, consider its graphics and any other qualities that may appeal to collectors and decorators.

Beginning in the 1980s collectors began placing a value on the boxes in which objects were marketed. Great graphics are what makes a box collectible. Information found only on the box about the manufacturer, pattern name, etc., also creates value. Some boxes, for example, cereal boxes, department store boxes, hat boxes, oatmeal boxes, tobacco tins, etc., became collectibles in their own right.

In some cases the box is worth more than the object found inside. The box for a character watch, for example, Mickey Mouse or Roy Rogers, can triple or quadruple the value of the watch. Record album sleeves, especially from the psychedelic era, are often worth many times more than the records inside. With toy trains, the box is almost a requirement to make a sale. Indeed, the boxes themselves can fetch high prices. To a noncollector, the fact that an empty 1930s to 1950s Lionel train set box can command a hundred dollars or more, seems ridiculous, but it is important to know about this before you choose to toss the boxes of items you find.

Completeness

An object is complete when it has all the parts with which it started out in life. A teapot missing a lid is not complete. A boxed board game missing two of its playing cards is not complete. An object has to be complete to have any chance of selling at its maximum reuse value.

Determining if an object is complete is not an easy task. It is made easier when a parts list exists or is included in play or use instructions. When these do not exist, use common sense. If you have an electric coffeepot with lid and cord, chances are it is complete. If you have an action figure removed from its blister pack, chances are it is not complete unless you have the accessories that came with it.

In mathematics class you learned the equation that the whole is equal to the sum of the parts. In certain parts of the antiques, collectibles, and desirables field, the sum of the parts may be greater than the whole. I once spoke with an individual who bought modern action figures, took them out of their packaging, and offered the parts separately on the Internet. Much to my surprise, and his initially, he recovered two to three times his original purchase price per object.

TIP When going through your things or those in an estate, set aside a box into which you put the "oddball" pieces you come across. Eventually you may find the appropriate mate, thus creating a complete piece.

Because most objects are mass produced, acquiring parts from one incomplete unit to make another incomplete unit complete does not present a problem. The goal is to reconstruct the unit as it was initially sold, and many collectors will be happy to purchase missing "odd parts" from you.

Local and Regional

Although the adage of "take an object back to its place of origin and double its value" no longer applies universally, local and regional values are still important. When an object was distributed and sold nationally, its local and regional value lessens.

The Internet, especially eBay, has strengthened the value of many objects with regional and local value, and enables sellers to reach buyers of local-interest items who may no longer live in the area. I grew up in Hellertown, Pennsylvania, and at least once a week do a "Hellertown" search on eBay. I have bought some great stuff including a second copy of my high school yearbook.

TIP When going through your things or those of an estate, set aside a box into which you put any objects that relate to any communities within a fifty-mile radius.

Local and regional collectors are potential buyers for a wide range of material including: any item with advertising; broadsides, histories, and other printed materials; objects related to or manufactured by local and regional businesses; objects associated with local and regional personalities and organizations; and postcards. This list barely scratches the surface.

One Generation

There are many questions collectors dread. One of the least favorite questions is: What's going to happen to all the stuff when the generation who grew up with it dies? This is an extremely relevant question to ask in the twenty-first century. The concept has impacted many collecting categories, especially in the ceramic and glass fields.

Traditional collectors and dealers continue to believe that every collecting category will eventually recycle. They have been waiting since the late 1940s for this to happen to copper luster ware. Market trends in the 1990s proved this wrong.

In the twenty-first century collecting the same object over two generations is considered terrific and over three generations spectacular. Most collecting categories, especially those focusing on late-nineteenth- and twentieth-century items, fall in the one generation and done category.

FACT Nothing has value unless buyers know what it is.

Want to test my theory? Answer the following four questions:

1) Who is William S. Hart?
2) What is peachblow?
3) What did Homer Laughlin make?
4) What is a Shmoo?

Let's see how you did:

1) Silent-film western cowboy movie star
2) An art glass that shades from an opaque pink tint to a deep rose
3) Dinnerware
4) A character from the *Li'l Abner* comic strip

If you are under fifty and had even one answer right, I take my hat off to you. If you answered all four correctly, my guess is you are living in a senior citizen retirement community. If you are under forty and did not get even one right, do not worry. I fully understand that you could not care less. This is the very point I am trying to make. **Value is generational.**

There are exceptions to the one-generation rule. The two most obvious are collecting categories focused on international brands, for example, Baccarat, Lalique, and Wedgwood, and investment-grade items, such as the high end of the comic book and sports card markets.

In the first decade of the twenty-first century, the hot collecting decades are the 1960s and 1970s, with material beginning to creep in from the 1980s. The 1950s are passé. Forget about the 1920s and the 1930s.

TIP Your grandchildren's toys may be more marketable than your toys. Do not throw out those Transformers or My Little Pony items.

There is a direct relationship between desirability and one-generation collectibles. The value of a generation's memorabilia and household furnishings reaches its collecting value peak when the average age of members of that generation is between fifty and sixty-two years of age. Value starts decreasing when the average

age exceeds sixty-two. Unfortunately most individuals wait until their seventies before they sell. Alas the value peak is by then a distant memory.

Investment

In every collecting category, there is a group of objects I describe as ultimate units and upper-echelon pieces. Ultimate units are the top five to ten objects in the category most desired by collectors. Obviously they also tend to be the most valuable. Upper-echelon pieces comprise the next fifty to one hundred objects based on desirability.

A collecting category's market strength is measured by how its common (low-end) and middle-market pieces perform. The high-end pieces, that is, ultimate units and upper echelon objects, always do well. A collecting category can be weak at its base and still see substantial growth among its high-end objects. Buyers view these items as investment-grade material and purchase them as commodities and not as objects to be loved and revered. They are held until the market increases significantly and then sold.

♠ | FACT It takes deep pockets to participate in the high end of the market.

The odds of you owning a high-end investment object are slim. Yet it does happen. Just watch the *Antiques Roadshow.*

The Story

Buyers love stories. Although reason dictates that a great story should not influence value, it does. Stories add personality to mass-produced objects. They help distinguish that object from all others like it.

The more documentation you provide about the objects you want to sell, the easier it is going to be to sell them. A piece of common jewelry accompanied by a picture of a family member wearing it will sell more quickly than if the picture was not present.

TIP The story you tell needs to be plausible. Today's buyers are sophisticated. They can spot a concocted story in heart-beat.

The Only Value That Counts

Are you more confused now than when you started reading this chapter? I hope not. However you now know that dozens of different factors in thousands of possible combinations determine the worth of what you will keep, sell, or toss.

Is there a way to simplify all this? Fortunately the answer is yes.

When I teach individuals how to buy antiques and collectibles successfully, I instill in them the concept that the only price that counts is the one they are willing to pay.

Since you face a choice of keep, buy, or toss, a slightly different approach is needed. The only price that counts is one that makes you happy.

This is no time for woulda, coulda, and shoulda. It is time to make those tough decisions. If your decision is to sell, the only successful conclusion is the sale of the object.

This chapter's goals were threefold: To help you (1) better understand the value of the objects you plan to keep, (2) set realistic prices for the objects you plan to sell, and (3) understand that you should toss less and sell more.

Now to the task at hand—facing a house full of objects.

CHAPTER TWO

Creating a Disposal Plan

A T first glance the task seems overwhelming. A lifetime of treasures stares you in the face. It makes no difference whether you, you and your spouse, your parents, or a relative assembled them. The pile is a big one. It goes on for room after room. There may be yet more possessions in sheds, rental storage units, and vacation homes. Americans love to accumulate, and sorting through such a wealth of items is daunting.

But fear not—the task you face is not as scary as it seems. It is time to roll up your sleeves and attack it. If you follow the guidelines in *Sell, Keep, or Toss?*, it will all be over in six months or less. Repeat the previous sentence now and continue for the next thirty days.

This chapter will help you create a plan for clearing out a home, whether due to downsizing or a death. Although the emotional issues are very different, many of the practical concerns are the same. Make sure to keep an eye out for the advice that is specific to your situation.

TIP Resist the temptation to start by tossing. There is gold in the things you think are junk.

Downsizing

If you are downsizing, acquire the floor plan of your new residence and study the room plans. Check to see what storage space is available, both on-site and nearby. You will want to take what you need, but do not overdo it. A move is a fresh start. You may want some new things—things you can buy with the cash you received from selling some of your possessions prior to your move.

Contact movers and get rough estimates of the cost to transport your goods from one location to another. The cost to move your daughter's piano, which has not been used for years, may not be justifiable, in which case it is better to sell it before you move.

If you are moving several hundred miles away, visit the area and check out the local auctions and antiques malls. Some things sell better in one region than another. It might pay to move some items and sell them in your new location.

Talk with your family members and friends about your upcoming move. There is a risk in doing this. You may get more advice and requests to help than you are prepared to handle. Just remember, you are in control. Better your family and friends know in advance than after the fact.

Preplan

After consulting and dealing with immediate family considerations, devote one week to planning how you will proceed. Preplanning will shorten the task by months. It will allow you to move systematically and rationally. Mistakes are made when things are done in haste or panic.

DETERMINE WHO IS IN CHARGE

Someone needs to be in charge. The person needs to be strong willed, capable of making decisions, able to resist outside pressures, a diplomat, and impervious to criticism. Much as you may wish it otherwise, there are usually a few individuals who will not like and may even resent some of the decisions made.

When a couple is involved in downsizing, both need to be involved in the decision-making process. If the couple has been together their entire married life, this makes the downsizing process easier. Today many marriages involve second, third, and even fourth partners. This opens the door to the my stuff, your stuff, and our stuff decisions. While I am not recommending such spouses go to sensitivity training before beginning the downsizing process, it is important to consider that different objects may have greater significance to one partner. Downsizing is not an easy process, especially when every item considered has a personal story attached to it.

DETERMINING HOW MUCH TIME YOU HAVE

Time is money. Time also is a friend. There is a direct correlation between the amount of time you spend in the preplanning and implementation process and the amount of money you will receive for the objects you decide not to keep.

FACT Individuals always underestimate the amount of time required for downsizing or the dispersal of an estate.

If you are downsizing, chances are you are living with your personal property. There is no travel time involved, unless a vacation home is involved. If you are working or volunteering, you can complete the planning process in the evening. If your children are helping you downsize, they may have to travel some distance. If this is the case, set aside specific dates and times for the preplanning and implementation process.

When considering how much time you have available, think in time blocks of two to three days and full weeks. The best decisions about what to keep, sell, or toss are made with a few days of rest between the preliminary, middle, and final choice processes.

Developing a Plan to Get the Job Done

Deciding what to sell, keep, or toss and then implementing the decisions can be done in a minimum of three to a maximum of six months. The plan to accomplish this task should take no more than one to two weeks to develop.

A downsizing plan can be completed in two to three months. The settlement of an estate takes longer. Three months is the minimum. Four to six months is ideal. Any time spent past six months is wasteful.

TWO-MONTH (EIGHT-WEEK) DOWNSIZING PLAN

Talking about downsizing is one thing. Actually doing it is another. It makes no sense to develop a downsizing plan until you know where you are going. Only start the planning process once you are holding the room plan of your new home, be it a smaller house, condominium, or rental apartment, in your hands.

Devote week one to talking with family and friends. Your children will need time to get over the shock. They never thought you would leave the family homestead, no matter how much advance warning you gave them. The home you are leaving is loaded with memories, and you are the one dislodging them.

Set aside week two to talk with your immediately family and determine what things, if any, they would like if you decide to sell or toss as opposed to keep. "My children do not want anything," my clients often tell me. My immediate response is: "Did you ask? If you did not, how do you know?" Most individuals tell me they are pleasantly surprised by the responses they get when they do ask.

You may receive a request from one or more child or grandchild for a specific piece. Take notes. Do not make decisions or promises.

The time for this is later. Right now you are the most important person. Your name belongs at the top of every list.

◆ FACT You come first.

Also work with your spouse during week two to make a list of those objects that mean the most to you. Hopefully these are family heirlooms and objects with rich personal stories attached to them. Share the stories with each other. It is okay to be maudlin during week two. It is not all right after week four.

Prepare the list of things you are going to keep in week three. Make the selection based on the following three questions:

1) Does it mean so much to me that I cannot bear to part with it?
2) Is it something I need for day-to-day living?
3) Is it worth paying the price to move?

Be generous to yourself on the first round of identifying those items with which you cannot part. If you are typical, your list will contain two to three times more items than will fit into your new living space. Once completed, put the list aside and return to it in week five.

Day-to-day living requires everything from pots and pans to towels and linens. Over time people tend to acquire far more than they need. Start the culling process immediately. Downsizing means living more sparsely.

◆ TIP Eliminate redundant kitchen tools. You will probably be shocked to find that you have three corkscrews and six vegetable peelers in your drawer. You need take only one of each to your new home.

Downsizing will change your entertainment pattern. Holiday celebrations will most likely move from your house to those of your children or grandchildren, so perhaps it is time to move the holiday china to the home of the child who will host future Thanksgiving dinners. You will likely entertain out more than you will in. Understanding the lifestyle that you are about to create is critical to determining what you will keep and what will be left behind to be sold.

Unless you are going to rent a moving van and move yourself, you will be hiring a moving company to transport your goods from one location to another. Although several variables influence the cost of a move, distance and weight are the two most important considerations.

Do you want to pay to move five-year-old towels? Would it not make more sense to buy new? The cost to move a washer and dryer may exceed the cost to purchase a new washer and dryer when you arrive at your new home.

TIP If you do not plan to use it, do not plan to move it.

Spend week four evaluating what is left. Divide the remaining material into the sell and toss pile. Directions on how to do this appear in chapter four. If you are impatient, jump forward, read chapter four, and then return here.

Also use week four to acquire packing material. It is more efficient to pack as you go than to postpone it until the final two weeks. Boxes and packing material can be purchased at any office supply store. If your home is typical, you will require a lot of packing material. Compare prices. Even so, expect some sticker shock.

FACT There are plenty of free boxes available at liquor stores. These boxes are sturdy and of a size that is easy to handle.

Begin week five by taking a second look at your keep list. The time has arrived for the tough decision. If you take more than you can use, you will have to rent a storage unit at your new location. Think twice, three times, even four times before deciding to take this approach. It is better to get rid of things now rather than later. However, if you simply cannot do this mentally, take the excess with you and rent a storage unit at your new location. Do NOT rent it at your existing location. You will not return as often as you think.

Using the room sketches of your living environment, prepare a layout of how you will use the major pieces you are taking. Avoid cramming pieces into a room. Leave some open space. This layout will greatly assist the movers and you when you arrive at the new location.

Evaluate the small items, everything from family photographs to clothing, on your take list. Do you have sufficient storage space in cabinets, closets, and the furniture you are taking? If not, some of it has to be eliminated.

If you are headed down to warmer climes and your children are located much farther north, consider storing your winter things at one of their homes. After all they are the primary reason you are going to head back north. Skis are of little use in Florida.

Use week six to decide the methods you are going to use to dispose of the things you have decided to sell. You know you are on the right track when you are considering a multiplicity of sale options and dividing your sell items into what works best in each.

In evaluating the items you have set aside to sell, you may conclude there are some that are better donated than sold. This is the week to take them to the various charities you have selected.

You are in the home stretch. Use week seven to sell or place your items for sale with the sale venues you have selected. The plan is simple. Get rid of the stuff. The goal is to reach the end of week eight with only those items you plan to take with you to your new living quarters.

As week seven ends, you most likely will face the prospect that some of the items you hoped to sell did not. Your decision at this point is simple. Donate them or toss them?

Week seven also is when you tell the children, relatives, and friends to pick up the things you are passing on to them. Be firm. Come get it, or we are getting rid of it—no ifs, ands, or buts. Children have a tendency to ask their parents to keep objects promised to them until they have room for them. The simple truth is that the children never find the room, burdening the parents with storage and/or moving issues. If someone wants something bad enough, you have every right to insist they pick it up at your convenience. If they do not, do not hesitate to consider the question: How much did they really want it?

The final tossing process marks the beginning of week eight. Actually you should have been tossing items as you went through the keep or sell decision-making process. Toss now with a vengeance. You do not want it. You cannot find a buyer for it.

Do not be surprised in you feel depressed. In fact, expect it. Ridding yourself of the bulk of your lifetime treasures is hard. Each item you sell or toss goes with your personal memories attached to it.

FACT Allow yourself time to grieve.

At the conclusion of the eighth week, you are left with the objects that you will take with you to your new home. Do not be in a hurry to move. No one said you had to do this the moment your downsizing effort was completed. Take a few days, even a few weeks, to adjust to living with what you decide to keep.

Accept the fact that you probably sold or tossed a few things you should have kept. Do not fret. You can replace them.

Far more likely is your discovery that some of the things you thought were essential turned out not to be. One additional quick round of sell or toss resolves the problem.

Move when you are ready, not before. However, it is better to move to your new home earlier rather than later. The empty spaces created by the objects you sold or tossed will bother you.

TIP Once you have moved, do not go back to your previous house. It is never the same. I know you do not believe this. But time will prove me right. Reserve your visits home for family and friends. These never change.

Settling an Estate

When faced with deciding what personal property involved in an estate to sell, keep, or toss, make a four-month plan. If you complete the four-month plan in six months, give yourself a pat on the back and party. There is always slippage in an estate-dispersal-of-personal-property plan. Do not be surprised when it occurs. Accept it, but do your best to control it.

First Things First

Devote the first two weeks to family and friends. Take time to grieve. This is an emotional, not a rational, period. Do not begin the dispersal decision-making process until you have your emotions partially in check. You will never have them fully in check throughout this entire process—personal memories coupled with pressure from a wide variety of sources, for example, family and legal matters, will make that impossible—but taking time first to grieve will make things easier. Make it clear to everyone that nothing will be dispersed until the will is read and sufficient time allowed to develop a plan that respects the wishes of the deceased.

TIP Accept the fact that emotions play a role in every decision you make. When they become overwhelming, walk away and do your best to get them under control before making a decision.

Who Is In Charge?

Normally one thinks of an executor of an estate as a family member or members, usually a child or children of the deceased. This is not always the case. Attorneys and bank trust officers are often appointed as executors. If this is the case, the family heirs should appoint a spokesperson to work with the executor to see that the family's wishes and needs are respected.

While the ideal situation is to have the deceased select one family member as their executor, this is often not the case. The deceased cannot choose one child over another. Hence he or she appoints them all and leaves it to them to work things out.

Dispersal of a deceased's personal property by committee is difficult and can lead to tension within the family. But if family members can work together, it can shorten the task considerably. Having a single executor also runs the risk that his decisions will favor him and his heirs.

When there are multiple executors, consider dividing the estate settlement tasks. *Sell, Keep, or Toss?* deals with the disposal of personal property. Other tasks include locating and arranging the dispersal of liquid financial assets such as stocks, bonds, savings accounts, etc., and preparing and arranging to sell or transfer title to the house and car.

There is often considerable pressure on the executor(s) to disperse goods immediately. This can come from relatives who have traveled some distance and want to take what they expect to inherit home with them to avoid a trip back, friends to whom the deceased has "promised" something, and rival heirs.

Hopefully the deceased prepared a will and named an executor(s). If so, the executor(s) should engage the services of an attorney, either the one who prepared the deceased's will or one of his/their own choosing. After arranging a reading of the will, the attorney will file the appropriate legal documents allowing the executors to act.

If no will exists, the apparent legal heirs should engage the services of an attorney to explain the prevailing laws of the state in which the deceased lived. Once the correct executor(s) is determined, the planning process can proceed.

FACT Laws vary from state to state. Do not assume you know the law. Hire an attorney.

Determining How Much Time You Have

Many executors do not live near the home of the deceased. They have to maximize their time. They have no choice. The number of vacation days an employee receives is limited. Utilizing them all to settle an estate means a year of all work and no play. The situation is easier to manage if the executor(s) is retired.

FACT An executor is entitled to an administration fee for managing the estate. Most do not take it. They should.

Deciding what to sell, keep, or toss and then implementing the decisions can be done in a minimum of three to a maximum of six months. The plan to accomplish this task should take no more than one to two weeks to develop.

If the deceased lived in a rental unit, it may be necessary to condense the process in order to save rental costs or meet a lease obligation. If the estate is confined to a small apartment or condominium, the process can be accelerated. Allow the full complement of time when dealing with any living space over a thousand square feet.

Securing the Personal Property of the Deceased

As the executor(s) of an estate, you have the responsibility to secure the personal property of the deceased until it is dispersed. Take the following steps:

1. Make certain you have a security person at the house during the viewing and funeral. These are prime times when robbers strike.

2. Immediately photograph or videotape every room in the house. This becomes a permanent record of what was in the home.

3. If no one will be living in the house, install a security system that includes fire as well as intruder protection. Talk to the neighbors and ask them to keep an eye on the house. Inform the local police that no one will be living in the house and ask them to step up their patrols. Make certain that all these individuals know how to contact you if there is an emergency.

4. Call the company that insures the house and contents and make certain the coverage remains in effect. Change the mailing address for billing to your address.

5. Call the telephone, electric, and heating companies to make certain these services continue. Again change the mailing address for billing to your address.

6. Change the locks on the door. You have no idea to whom the deceased may have given keys.

7. Cancel all cleaning services.

8. If one does not already exist, hire a service to do outside maintenance, for example, cut the lawn, rake the leaves, shovel snow, etc. Even though no one is home, you want the house to have a lived-in look.

9. Install several devices that turn lamps on and off in the evening.

10. Gather all jewelry, especially pieces made from precious and semiprecious gems, gold and silver coins, objects made of precious metals, that is, gold, platinum, and sterling silver, remove them from the premises, and place them in a highly secure environment.

11. Cancel the newspaper.

12. Make arrangements with the United States Postal Service to hold mail at the local post office.

Securing the Estate

Secure the deceased's home and personal property. Some steps, such as making certain there are people in the house continuously for several days following the deceased's death, need to be done immediately. Others can be postponed until after the grieving process. All should be in place by the end of the first month.

Use the second half of the first month to walk through the home with family and friends. Share stories, talk about the objects.

Begin compiling a list of objects people want. DO NOT MAKE ANY PROMISES. Most importantly do not allow anyone to remove anything. There is a time and place for everything, and this is neither the time nor place.

Arrange for the reading of the deceased's will two to three weeks after the burial. The will specifies who will act as executor or executors. If there is no will or no will can be found, consult with an attorney to determine how the state law applies in respect to appointing an executor and determining who the lawful heirs are.

The will may contain the deceased's wishes in respect to how he or she wanted specific pieces of personal property distributed. This information may be found in the body of the will or as an attachment. An executor is bound by the terms of the will. An attachment is viewed in some states as merely a recommendation. The executor has the ability to change its wishes. Again, ask an attorney to explain the prevailing laws.

TIP Safe-deposit box information is generally found in a desk drawer, top drawer of a dresser (where the jewelry is kept), or strongbox/safe.

If the deceased had a safe-deposit box, make arrangements to obtain access to its contents. Normally a spouse has access without an official estate document authorizing access. An executor may not. Once again an attorney can advise you on the prevailing laws. It is customary for bank officers to make an inventory of the contents of a safe-deposit box which then becomes part of the estate's records. Everything from stocks and bonds to cash to jewelry is recorded. If a copy of a written appraisal of some of the personal property of the deceased is present, it becomes part of the estate's record.

One of the four months has passed. While it may seem as though you accomplished little, you actually have accomplished a great deal. You have allowed yourself to accept the death of the deceased, secured the property, had the will read, probated the will and secured the appropriate documents allowing you to act as the executor of the estate, talked with family and friends to understand their wishes and desires, and gained an appreciation for the task ahead.

The dispersal of personal property in an estate is only one step of dozens involved in settling an estate. The executor(s)' many responsibilities include, but are not limited to, arranging for and paying for the burial, probating the will, locating and implementing insurance policies, closing checking and savings accounts, opening an estate account, arranging for the liquidation or transfer of stocks and bonds, and arranging for the sale of the house and any vehicles owned by the deceased.

MONTH TWO

Begin the second month by determining what help you will need to assist you in the dispersal of the deceased's personal property. Do you need the services of a personal property appraiser? If family heirlooms from multiple generations dominate the estate or the deceased was a collector, consider engaging the services of a personal property appraiser to do an initial evaluation. If the deceased acquired most of the objects new during his lifetime, the services of a personal property appraiser are probably not necessary.

Before making a specific decision, you need to get an overview of the amount and type of personal property with which you will be working. This means opening every drawer, checking out every closet, unpacking and looking inside the boxes in the attic and basement, and checking the loft in the garage. Doing this is time-intensive. The more help available, the faster the time goes. Set a goal of one week to get everything out and examined.

◆ FACT Elderly people often hide money. Favorite hiding places include shoes/shoe boxes, underneath the paper liners in drawers and closets, under carpets, pockets of suits and dresses hung in the master closet, and cans and jars in the kitchen and basement. Toss nothing without a thorough inspection.

You will never get this task done in a week if you stop and think about the story behind each object you are handling. This is not the time to leaf through the family photo albums, reminisce about childhood toys, school mementos, or vacation souvenirs, or tell stories about parents, grandparents, and great-grandparents. There will be ample time to do this once the objects are dispersed.

In the middle of the second month, identify and put aside those items specified in the will or attachment designated to go to a specific individual. It is still not time to release them. Tell the new owners to be patient a little longer.

Family before friends, friends before outsiders is the best rule to follow in determining the objects not designated in the will that will be kept and dispersed rather than sold or tossed. Many factors play a role in the decision-making process, including whether children and grandchildren will be treated equally or if division will be by family, deciding who will eventually receive an object if more than one person has expressed interest, and, if money is needed to settle the estate or for an heir, what can be dispersed without charge and what needs to be sold.

As the second month ends, the keep list should be finalized. It is time once again to consider bringing in a personal property appraiser. If the list contains a high number of antiques and collectibles, consider asking the appraiser to do a written appraisal.

This establishes a cost basis for the new owners should they ever decide to sell the objects they have inherited. Second, it provides the executor with a set of figures he can use to adjust any financial inequities between the fair market value of the objects going to one person versus the value of those going to others. If the estate contains few antiques and collectibles, the services of a personal property appraiser may not be needed.

FACT Today heirs tend to be more interested in a balanced financial distribution than a one-for-one distribution of objects.

MONTH THREE

The third month begins by asking the heirs to remove the objects they have inherited. This provides room for the major task ahead, making the keep, sell, or toss decision for the remaining objects.

It also allows the executor to begin investigating the many methods—auction, estate sale, garage sale, Internet, or outright purchase— available to dispose of those objects designated for sale. These options will be addressed in greater detail in later chapters. It is not fair to an auctioneer or estate sale manager to invite them into an estate and then tell them you cannot sell this, or this, or this, or this, etc., because it is staying in the family. When a potential seller is called in to look, he should see only what he will be asked to sell.

By the middle of the third month, the executor should have a dispersal plan in place. Once the methods of sale have been selected, the individuals selected to execute them should be consulted for recommendations of what to sell and what to toss.

Using multiple sale methods maximizes the value received for an estate's personal property. However, more often than not, a single method of disposal is selected because it is quick, convenient, and fits the amount of time the executor has to devote to the estate's personal property. If this is the case, so be it.

FACT A house and property that is "broom clean" and ready to sell is the primary goal. There is usually more value in the real estate than in the personal property.

If the auction method is one of the sale approaches, have the auctioneer remove the property he can sell as the third month ends. House sales, that is, selling from the porch or yard of a house, are becoming rarer and rarer. In the twenty-first century most auctioneers sell out of their own auction gallery or a rented venue such as a local fire hall.

MONTH FOUR

If the estate sale method is selected, it should take place early in the fourth month. The same holds true for a garage sale. This also is the time to deliver those items that will be donated to institutions or given to charity.

As the fourth month ends, the deceased's home should be empty. It is time for the executor to turn the home over to a real estate agent and devote his remaining time to the other aspects required to settle the estate.

Is it possible to accomplish the dispersal of a deceased's personal property in four months? Absolutely! Is it likely to happen? Absolutely not!

Just like antiques and collectibles values, goals are guidelines, not absolutes. Strive to achieve them. Be understanding when you do not. Most importantly, stay focused. There is light at the end of the tunnel.

CHAPTER THREE

Getting the Right Help

GETTING the right help is not as easy as it appears. A generous offer to help may not be as generous as it seems.

When preparing to downsize or to settle an estate, you are likely to find that you have more offers to help than you need as opposed to too few. The reasons are many. Curiosity and the chance to get "first pick" are dominant ones. Many individuals who offer to help may place their own interests above those whom they are helping

TIP Be suspicious of all offers to help. Question the generosity and motivation behind every offer until you are satisfied with the answers.

Take a skeptical approach when evaluating offers to help. This approach may run counter to everything you believe about humankind, but better to be in control than vulnerable.

Your job is to select and work with individuals whose only interest is your interest and/or that of the estate. Your interests must come first. Your needs must be paramount. The professionals you engage must remain neutral and exhibit the highest of ethical standards. The family members, neighbors, and friends you allow to help must be unselfish in mind as well as in heart. Culling these individuals from the myriad of individuals who want to help is no easy task.

Professional Help

There are many skilled professionals—accountants, attorneys, appraisers, and/or estate planners—whom you may wish to consult and employ. You can downsize or settle an estate without consulting or employing any of these individuals, but doing so carries risks. It is wise to engage those professionals who have skills you do not possess. Their knowledge will save you time and money over the long term by helping you avoid costly mistakes.

The goal is to do it right the first time—once and done. Many of the decisions you make cannot be revisited and reversed.

Estate Attorney

An estate attorney is the one professional whose services are an absolute necessity. Few question the need for an estate attorney when settling an estate. However, downsizing is also similar to settling an estate, especially when it involves distributing family heirlooms among family members and friends. Distribution always has tax consequences, whether stocks and bonds, cash gifts, or personal property.

FACT While many people try to avoid the tax responsibilities involved with the distribution of personal property by not reporting the personal property of an estate, do not be one of them.

Attorneys specialize. Many people have a family attorney, an attorney who handles their general legal needs and may have even drawn up their will. When downsizing or settling an estate, you need an attorney who specializes in estate work.

Ask your family attorney to recommend several estate specialists. If your family attorney indicates that he feels adequate to meet your needs, ask him for references from people he has helped.

If you do not have a family attorney or your needs are in an area distant from your home, seek recommendations from the local or regional bar association. You can try searching the Internet, but keep in mind that firms and attorneys pay the search engines to give their listings priority.

Keep it simple and local. Start with the recommendations from your family attorney and the local/regional bar association.

It pays to compare. This may be a cliché, but it applies here.

Knowledge of state and federal estate law is essential. However, it is also essential to have someone you can trust and with whom you feel comfortable. You do not want to have a clash of wills and personalities with your attorney during the settlement process. There is enough potential for this elsewhere. Engage an attorney with whom you are compatible and whose philosophy of accounting is identical to your philosophy. The law is the law. While subject to interpretation, its variables fall in a very narrow confine.

Meet any prospective attorney in his office. There should be no charge for the initial consultation. Do not be afraid to ask the attorney for his résumé and a list of references. Ask the attorney to describe the services he provides. Most importantly, ask him about his fee structure.

TIP Ask if the attorney is willing to accept a flat, fixed fee to handle the estate rather than a per-hour fee. You might be pleasantly surprised.

Unless there are extenuating circumstances, hire an attorney who charges an hourly fee or a flat fee. Avoid attorneys whose charges are based on a percentage of the estate. The estate should not be penalized because the person who created it was wealthy.

A skilled attorney should be able to provide you with a rough estimate of the number of hours involved in settling the estate. Consider establishing a review after a fixed number of hours, for example, fifteen, have been spent. Expect to be billed monthly.

Ask specifically how hourly fees are assessed. Are you charged for a short phone call, that is, less than five minutes? Is travel time billed at the same rate as research and writing time? If a junior partner or paralegal works on your estate are his or her hours billed at the same rate as the lead attorney? If you have lunch or dinner with your attorney and just pass the time of day rather than talk about the estate, does the attorney consider himself on the clock? Billing time ranges from five-minute to fifteen-minute intervals. It pays to know. Plan the time you spend with the attorney you hire accordingly.

Hourly charges are only one revenue source for the attorney. Other charges include filing fees, duplicating documents, long-distance phone calls, and mileage. These are standard charges and considered fair. However, beware of being nickeled and dimed to death.

American Bar Association

American Bar Association
321 North Clark Street
Chicago, IL 60610
(800) 285-2221
www.abanet.org

Finding an attorney: Go to the Web site, click on "Find Legal Help" on the home page. This takes you to a page featuring a map of the United States. Click on the appropriate state, which this brings up a page featuring a number of legal services, then click on "Lawyer Referral." This takes you to a list of the bar associations within the state.

The ABA Web site also features a "Lawyer Locator" button. Use this if you have the name of an attorney but do not know the address or phone number.

Do you need an estate attorney if you are downsizing? The answer is yes if you own a large amount of valuable personal property and are planning to distribute a portion of it at this time or if you plan to draw up a new will based on the results of your downsizing. The answer is no if your primary purposes is only estate planning. While some estate attorneys also offer estate planning services, an estate planner is an individual who also brings accounting and long-term financial management expertise to the table.

Accountant

If your personal estate or the estate for which you are acting as executor is large, you should consider engaging the services of an accountant as well as an estate attorney. An attorney's focus is on the law. An accountant's focus is on financial questions. Large firms specializing in estate work often have accountants on their staff.

If you have an established personal/business relationship with an accountant or accounting firm, you can continue to work with him or her. It is not necessary for the accountant to be on-site when settling an estate or downsizing.

TIP Hire an accountant who is a CPA, that is, a certified public accountant.

If you do not have an accountant, follow the same procedure you used to secure the services of an estate attorney. Do you prefer an accountant from a small firm, perhaps even a single-owner firm, or are you more comfortable with someone in a large firm?

Accountants divide into two types—conservatives and liberals. Both operate within the law. Do not hire any accountant who even remotely hints at bending the law to save you money. A conservative accountant stays well within established accounting principles. A liberal accountant pushes the boundaries. Are you willing to risk a state or federal review of your final estate settlement filings or do you want to avoid a review at all cost? The decision is yours to make.

Make arrangements for your accountant and attorney to meet. They will need to consult and possibly even work together. Remember, both are engaged on a per-hour basis. In an effort to keep costs under control, ask them to inform you in advance of any interactions.

FACT Never allow anyone, professional or nonprofessional, to take an object or objects from an estate or downsizing effort in lieu of hourly fees.

Appraiser

When hiring an appraiser for downsizing or estate purposes, ideally you need an appraiser trained in valuing both appreciating and depreciating personal property. Appreciating personal property is property that tends to increase in value over time. This category includes antiques, fine art, and collectibles. Depreciating personal property is property that loses value through use. This broad category includes everything from electrical appliances, for example, dishwashers, refrigerators, etc., to pots and pans and other household goods. Many antiques, fine art, and collectibles appraisers have expertise only in appreciating personal property. They have little to no knowledge of depreciating personal property.

It is difficult to find a generalist appraiser capable of handling both types of personal property. Auctioneers have this ability, but come with risks. Finding an auctioneer whose primary interest is appraisal service and not using the appraisal to gain an inside entry to obtaining the final sale is extremely problematic.

You are most likely to hire an appraiser specializing in appreciating personal property. You want a person who can help you avoid throwing out objects that have potential resale value. In addition you want this person to help you identify in which sale venue you can obtain the prices he quotes.

FACT There are no federal or state agencies that license appraisers.

There are private appraisal organizations, such as the American Society of Appraisers (ASA) and International Society of Appraisers (ISA), that have their own certification programs. However do not confuse their certification with a federal or state licensing program. In the final analysis what counts is the ability of the appraiser to (1) identify and value objects properly and (2) conform to the Appraisal Foundation's Uniform Standards of Professional Appraisal Practice (USPAP) if a written appraisal is required. The Appraisal Foundation is a nonprofit educational organization that fosters professionalism in valuation by establishing and promoting professional appraisal standards and appraiser qualifications. It is not a membership organization.

FACT When considering hiring an appraiser, ask him about USPAP. If he does not know about USPAP, do not hire him.

Do you need a written appraisal? In the vast majority of cases, the answer is no. If the answer is yes, a preliminary nonwritten valuation prior to deciding what objects would be included in a written appraisal still makes a great deal of sense.

FINDING AN APPRAISER

Where do you find an appraiser with the skills and expertise you need? First, contact your local or regional historical societies and museums and ask whom they recommend. The reference librarian at your public library is another reliable source. Second, ask family and friends for names of appraisers they have used. Third, your

Appraisal Organizations

RECOMMEND

American Society of Appraisers
PO Box 17265
Washington, DC 20071
(703) 478-2228
www.appraisers.org

International Society of Appraisers
16040 Christensen Road, Ste. 102
Seattle, WA 98188
(206) 241-0359
www.isa-appraiser.org

OTHERS

Appraisers Association of America
386 Park Avenue S, Ste. 2000
New York, NY 10016-8804
(212) 889-5404
www.appraisersassoc.org

The National Association of Jewelry Appraisers
PO Box 6558
Annapolis, MD 21401
(401) 897-0889
www.najaappraisers.com

attorney usually has a list of names of individuals with whom he has worked in the past. If you do contact one of these references, check if the attorney expects a referral fee for passing along the name. There is nothing illegal about this practice, but you should be informed of it. Finally, consult the yellow page listings in one or more of your local phone directories. Start your search by asking those appraisers with the initials ASA or ISA after their names to send you their résumés.

TIP Focus on the qualifications of the appraiser. Make certain they have the knowledge to appraise your objects.

Ask the appraiser to present you with a list of his qualifications. Focus specifically on the type of objects that he is capable of appraising. It makes no sense to use an appraiser of Native American objects to value a houseful of ceramics, furniture, glass, utilitarian goods, etc.

Asking for a list of references from an appraiser is tricky. Professional appraisers are sticklers when it comes to client confidentiality. They are extremely reluctant to release the names of any of their clients. You should insist on the same courtesy.

FACT The ability to know how to write an appraisal report, the focus of training for most appraisal associations, is no substitute for object identification and years of field experience.

Talk to more than one appraiser. Again find an individual in whom you have trust and who has a personality that makes it fun to work with him.

Engage the appraiser on a per-hour basis. Do not, repeat DO NOT, agree to pay for services based on a percentage of the final appraisal value or allow the appraiser to take one or more objects in exchange for services.

Tell the appraiser up front that he will not be allowed to buy any object that he appraises. It is unethical even to make such a request. The appraiser's focus has to be on serving you as a client. His goal is to provide the best advice, especially if you want to maximize the dollar return from selling objects.

The appraiser will ask you what you intend to do with the information he provides. Be honest. Your answer affects the value he assigns. If you plan to sell your objects at auction, the appraiser will provide you with an estimate of the hammer price. If you plan to distribute the objects among family, he may decide to value them halfway between wholesale and retail. If you are planning to donate one or more objects to charity, he is obligated by law to provide "fair market" value.

Do not hesitate to ask the appraiser where you can obtain the values he assigns to objects. A competent appraiser should provide you with a variety of selling choices.

Do not blame the appraiser if you do not like the values he assigns. You are paying him for his opinion, whether it is an opinion you like or not. The best appraiser provides values that are realistic and conservative. He would rather a client be pleasantly surprised than disappointed when a sale takes place.

Some appraisers also offer management services, especially in the dispersal of the appreciating property found in an estate. If you hire the person who appraised your objects to provide these services, continue to pay him on an hourly basis.

FACT Many antiques and collectibles auctioneers and dealers offer a finder's fee to a person who brings a client to them. Make it clear to any appraiser you hire that you wish to be informed if this is the case.

While allowing an appraiser who is managing the dispersal of a collection to accept a finder's fee in lieu of accepting an hourly payment from the client is a cost-cutting method, it is risky. In many cases the finder's fee far exceeds the hourly fee the appraiser/manager would have been paid. Realistically the appraiser/manager should be negotiating the best sales deals possible for his client. If there is a finder's fee, it belongs to the client or serves to reduce the portion of any sales cost borne by the client.

A skilled appraiser's rates are equivalent to those of an accountant or attorney. When the appraiser's rates are well below these standards, think twice. The old adage of "you get what you paid for" applies.

WALK-THROUGH APPRAISAL

Although not a standard service, consider engaging the services of a professional appraiser on an hourly basis to do a simple walk-through of the house and offer his opinions of what he sees. The appraiser walks a house from attic to basement, commenting on those objects he thinks have strong resale value. When done he sits down with the client and discusses disposal and other options. A walk-through appraisal does not make official statements about the value of specific objects—it merely identifies those that are worth selling and offers sales options. For most homes, a walk-through appraisal will be sufficient.

The owner or executor is encouraged to videotape or tape record the process. Some make notes. Others place Post-it notes on objects as the appraisal proceeds.

A good appraiser can complete a walk-through appraisal in one to two hours. Of course, larger homes may take longer—I have done some that have taken up to four hours.

■ | FACT | A little preparation can save time and money.

Prior to the arrival of the appraiser, remove everything from drawers, closets, storage containers, etc. Place objects on beds, dressers, tables, or wherever there is space. You do not want to pay the appraiser to stand around while you unpack things. Make certain there is adequate lighting. Have flashlights available. A bright sunny day is the best time to do a walk-through appraisal.

Do not be embarrassed to show the appraiser the attic, basement, garage, and any sheds. He has seen it all and more. Piles and dirt are commonplace when doing walk-through appraisals. Allow the appraiser to poke around. He will open cabinets and drawers. He is trained to know where to look. Expect him to ask plenty of questions, especially if he does not see what he expects to see.

When the walk-through is done, the appraiser will sit down with the client and review what he has seen. If the client is interested in selling, the appraiser should recommend six or more sales alternatives, exploring the pros and cons of each. If pieces are going to be kept, discuss with the appraiser the cost of having a written appraisal made of them. Also ask the appraiser to discuss insurance considerations involving the pieces that are retained.

WRITTEN APPRAISAL

Written appraisals are extremely helpful when property is being transferred, and are a must when the home contains many objects of great value. First and foremost, they provide a cost basis for the new owner, that is, the value of the object when the person acquired it. When an object is passed from one person to the next without an appraisal and the proper tax documentation, the cost basis to that person is zero.

Written appraisals take time. A good appraiser can list between twenty and twenty-five objects per hour when done to USPAP standards. Written appraisals are research appraisals. Expect the appraiser to spend one hour researching and preparing the final appraisal for each hour spent in the house doing the listings.

FACT The time to prepare written appraisals is measured in days and not hours.

One method of saving money is to restrict the number of items valued under five hundred dollars that are listed and concentrate on the more valuable items. Consider including a sampling of the lesser valued items as a means of showing the breadth of the holdings.

Written appraisals are generally based on replacement value, that is, what would have to be paid to replace the object with an identical or comparable object in the standard secondary retail marketplace, an antiques shop, or a show when considering antiques. Values differ regionally. The appraisal cover letter spells out the marketplace in which the objects are valued. If you are downsizing and moving some distance, consider asking the appraiser to prepare his written appraisal based on the objects' new location rather than their present location. If separate written appraisals are being done for heirs, the same applies.

TIP Photo document all objects that are part of a written appraisal.

Today most written appraisals are done on a computer. Insist that the appraiser provide you with a digital file of the listing. If the appraiser says no based on the premise that you might change something, stand firm in your demands. You paid for the document and you deserve a copy. When you have your objects appraised in the future, providing the appraiser with the digital file will reduce costs considerably. Do expect the appraiser to recheck the former appraiser's work. As much as appraisers hate to admit it, mistakes are made.

The time to have a written appraisal done is when you have already decided what to keep. Resist the temptation to do it immediately following a walk-through appraisal.

Bank Trust Officer

If you have no heirs and do not wish to appoint a friend or attorney as your estate executor, you may consider a bank trust officer. Bank trust officers serve an important role when the client's wealth is primarily in financial paper and accounts. However, a bank trust officer is a very poor choice if the client has a large number of family heirlooms or collections. Most bank trust officers have little to no experience with personal property, nor do they want any. When faced with the disposal of personal property, they seek the fastest means possible, either an auction or sale to a clean-out specialist.

● | TIP | Think twice, even three times, before making personal property the responsibility of a bank trust officer.

Nonprofessional Help

I love adages, and this book is filled with them. Here is another: Beware of friends bearing gifts. In this case the gift is an offer of time. Few offers to assist in the sell, keep, or toss decision-making process come without strings attached.

Heirs

Not all heirs are family. Not all family members are heirs. The will determines the executor or executors and the heirs. If there is no will, prevailing state laws will determine who serves as executor. The same applies to heirs.

Heirs have an immediate vested interest in the personal property. If there are multiple heirs and who is to get what is not clearly specified in the will, the decision-making process can quickly turn into a free-for-all.

Every heir wants his or her fair share. Defining "fair" is the problem. Does fair mean one for you and one for me or does fair mean an even dollar distribution once things are divided, the value of each heir's pile determined, and money added to rectify the imbalance if some piles are of lesser value?

Heirs frequently are concerned not only for themselves but for their respective immediate families. They are fighting for their own interests as well as those of their spouses, children, in-laws, and grandchildren.

Do not assume for one minute that the above applies only to the settlement of estates. When downsizing, property in the "distribute to the children" pile can evoke the same passions.

The key is the personal relationship the person who is downsizing or serving as executor has with the heirs or potential heirs. If they have worked well together in the past, accepting the offer to help is worth a try. However, be prepared to say no if an untenable situation develops.

FACT Be prepared to discover a side you never knew of a person when dealing with him or her on dispersal matters.

Family

Family divides into two groups—immediate and extended. Consider offers from immediate family members. Turn down all offers from extended family.

If downsizing limit the immediate family to your spouse. If you are a surviving spouse and serving as the executor, take a moment and consider if you can handle the dispersal alone. It may seem self-serving, but it generally eliminates the possibility of family conflicts. If you are going to involve your children and their spouses, either include or exclude them all. This is not the time to play favorites. If serving as an executor, widen the definition to brothers, sisters, and their spouses.

Avoid aunts and uncles. They are older than you. As such they think their opinions deserve not only consideration but acceptance simply based upon the fact that they are older than you. Aunts and uncles have difficulty accepting nieces and nephews as adults even when they are of retirement age.

Grandchildren and great-grandchildren belong in the background. If a child of the deceased has died, one or more grandchildren may ask to represent that family's interest in the decision-making process.

FACT The fewer individuals involved in the decision-making process the better. The best number is one.

A surprising choice for help may be a cousin or two with whom you are good friends and who know going into the process that nothing but thanks will be coming their way when the process is done.

The goal is to find helpers who are neutral, who have no interest financial or otherwise in the decision-making process of what to sell, keep, or toss.

Friends

On the surface friends appear to be completely neutral. Be suspicious, especially if the offer to help comes from a newly made friend.

In daily life we do not separate friends from acquaintances. When deciding what to sell, keep, or toss, this distinction must be made. Use this simple criterion to determine who is a friend and who is not: A friend is someone with whom I can share my innermost secrets and trust them not to say anything to anyone. Once you've applied that standard you are likely to find that your choices are few.

If involving a friend, make it clear that the only reward they can expect is thanks. Agreeing to help under these conditions is a good sign that the person is a true friend.

If settling an estate, do not accept help from anyone claiming to be a friend of the deceased. These people tend to be ruled by emotion and not reason. No matter what they claim, their primary goal is to position themselves to get an early look and, hopefully, in line for first pick.

Employees

Business is business. Downsizing and settling an estate is a family matter. Employees, whether from an individual's business or caregivers, do not belong in the decision-making process. No matter how well meaning, just say no.

Outsiders

You will be amazed at the amount of offers you will have from outsiders. These can range from a real estate agent engaged to sell the house to a fellow collector. I know several real estate agents whose homes are furnished with antiques that they bought from clients prior to public sale and even before distribution among family and friends. The pros and cons of involving a fellow collector or collectors are discussed in chapter five.

When settling an estate, expect offers to help from every club, social organization, or sports team to which the deceased belonged. Even though most offers are genuine, say no.

FACT When serving as an executor, maintain the appearance and propriety of neutrality at all costs.

The Right Help

What is the right help? The answer is simple. The right help is the help you and you alone decide you want. You make the decision. It is not dictated to you.

Before downsizing and before moving forward to settling an estate, take time to make a list of the help you feel you need. Keep the list small and manageable.

When assigning the names of individuals to the help chart you have prepared, pick those with the proper skills, those with whom you feel you can work, and, most importantly, those who will unquestionably accept your leadership.

Never add a person to the list for fear of offending them. A reasonable person will understand that you are in charge of assessing all offers to help and making the final decision. If a person becomes offended for being left off the list, he did not belong on the list in the first place.

Now that you have identified the help you need and picked the individuals who will work with you, it is time to start the sell, keep, or toss decision-making process.

CHAPTER FOUR

Organizing the Piles

C HAPTER two explained how to identify your disposal goals and develop a timetable. Hopefully you wrote them down. If not, take a minute or two and do it now. If you did, review them one final time before beginning.

Expect to alter your disposal goals as you proceed. Hidden treasures are a natural by-product of deciding what to sell, keep, or toss. Hidden treasures are those items stored in attics, closets, basements, etc., that you simply forgot. When they are rediscovered, they evoke such strong personal memories that there is no doubt whatsoever that they have to be kept.

FACT Expect any preliminary keep list to expand by twenty percent or more.

Your timetable is only a guide, a map designed to keep you focused and on the right track. Will it require an adjustment or two as you go through the disposal process? Absolutely! Keeping these adjustments minimal is one of the greatest challenges you will face. Staying focused is a must.

You also have selected those individuals who will help you in the disposal process. Contact them and provide them with a schedule of when their help will be needed. Do not schedule them until you need them. Think minimally rather than maximally. Although just the opposite would seem true, it is easier to request an increase in time if needed than telling a person who has set aside a prearranged amount of time that you do not need them.

TIP Minimize the number of times you handle an object.

Avoiding handling the same object numerous times is another major challenge in the disposal process. Think sell, keep, or toss from the first moment you pick up an object. Your first pile begins with the first object.

Not all first disposal decisions will stand. Second-guessing is an integral part of the disposal process. The ultimate goal is to create a series of piles that allows you the quick and efficient disposal of those objects that you are not planning to keep.

Sell, Keep, or Toss? is the title of this book. In creating your piles, think keep first, sell second, and toss third. This priority should remain paramount.

FACT Many of the objects traditionally tossed can be sold or donated. Only fools throw away money.

There is another priority you need to keep in the front of your mind. How do I maximize the financial return from the objects I am not keeping? Toss only what cannot be sold or donated. For example, most individuals bag and toss heavily worn clothing. Heavily worn clothing has scrap value. It may not be much, but it is something.

TIP Pack as you go, especially small items.

Make certain you have an adequate supply of boxes, packing material, sealing tape, and bags before you begin. Your goal is to pack as much as possible during your initial handling of the objects. Have plenty of felt-tip markers on hand. Do not set aside a box without marking in at least two locations on the box in permanent ink what is contained inside.

Visit your local stationery or office supply store and buy several packs of colored dot labels. Assign a color to each category, for example, red equals keep, and apply them to large pieces as a decision is made to sell, keep, or toss. Make certain the dot is large enough to write a name on it. Put the dot on a piece where it is visible, but where its glue will do the least possible damage. The assumption is that these dots will not remain on the pieces longer than six to eight weeks. If you are concerned about damage, you can use string-attached paper tags instead.

At this point in the dispersal process, your goal is merely to create piles. The selection of the method or methods to dispose of these piles is discussed in subsequent chapters.

Pile 1: Things You Want to Keep

This pile applies to individuals who are downsizing. If you are settling an estate, you might want to consider skipping this section and begin reading with Pile 2. However, if you are the sole executor of an estate, much of what follows applies to you. If in doubt, keep reading.

There are two basic types of objects you are going to keep. The first are those family and personal heirlooms that evoke strong memories. The second are those things you need for day-to-day living.

Ideally you acquired a floor plan of your new living accommodations during the planning process and did a major layout of the large pieces of furniture you plan to take with you. If you have not done this, do so immediately.

Chances are you discovered during the planning process that you want to take many more objects than will comfortably fit into your new home. While common sense indicates a "do not do this" approach, you do what is right for you. If you decided to take the extra objects and temporarily rent a storage unit in your new location, do so with the knowledge that this temporary storage unit may become costly and inconvenient over time.

◆ FACT Although rented initially on a temporary basis, storage rentals have a bad habit of becoming permanent rentals.

Leave the items you plan to keep in place until you are ready to move. Set aside areas for those you plan to sell or toss and begin placing items in these areas as you go along. Do not be concerned if your neat home looks a bit messy and disorganized. There is order in the confusion.

Family heirlooms are about memory. The memories in this case are your own personal memories. Use the intensity of your family memories as a guide. If your memories are strong, keep the object. If your memories are weak, consider retaining the object only if space is available.

If an object came down through the family but has little to no meaning to you, do not take it. You are not obligated to follow the wishes imposed on you by well-meaning ancestors. Further, avoid taking family heirlooms in the hope that "the kids will want them some day." This is the time you have chosen for them to give their "FINAL ANSWER" in respect to what they might want and not want.

Deciding what "big" pieces to keep is easy. They are visible. If you are not moving immediately, make a checklist. Apply a visible dot as suggested earlier.

Hopefully you already have your family financial and other paper records stored in storage boxes and file cabinets. If so, seal and mark these units. They are ready for transport.

Heirloom smalls range from family photographs to jewelry. This is not the time to sort through family photographs and slides. Move them to your new location and resolve to sort them there.

Take all heirloom jewelry. In terms of personal jewelry, take all jewelry made from precious metal and any that include precious and semiprecious gems. In respect to the rest, select the pieces to take based on how often you wear them.

TIP When was the last time that I wore/used this? Ask this question over and over again when trying to decide what to keep.

Gather the family ceramics, dinnerware, flatware, glass, linens, stemware, and other accessories. Balance your desire to take everything against these three questions:

1) When was the last time I used it?
2) Have the children or others expressed interest in it?
3) Is it something I can sell that will produce a handsome return?

Be honest with yourself. This is far more difficult than it seems. Chances are much of this material has been on display and not used in years, possibly even decades. If used, its use was selective, for example, entertaining and holidays. How much entertaining will you do and how many holidays will be spent at your new home? You may not like the answer you will get when asking this question, but ask it anyway.

FACT You own far more things than you need for basic day-to-day living.

The goal is to take only what you need. It is a goal that is almost impossible to meet. Pack your favorite day-to-day dinnerware, flatware, glassware, and kitchen items. Think in terms of one of everything. Chances are you have two to three sets of dishes. Do you really need the second or third set?

Apply a ten-year rule to appliances. A five-year rule is better, but you may feel that is too harsh. We still live in an era when older people expect things to last, at least for their lifetime if not beyond. Hence the recommended time is ten years. Even if a ten-year-old-plus appliance, whether a blender, sweeper, or otherwise, is still functional, consider selling it and buying a new one after you arrive at your new home.

Resist the temptation to keep necessities, for example, toilet paper, unused bottles of dishwasher detergent, etc. The cost to move them far exceeds the cost to replace them. If you simply cannot help yourself, pack one or two boxes with the "bear necessities" as Baloo the Bear noted in Disney's *Jungle Book*.

Now that you have designated those items you want to keep, it is time to decide what to do with the rest. If you are downsizing and not settling an estate, you may be tempted to skip the next section. Do not do this. It contains information you need.

Pile 2: Objects Designated for Distribution

As the executor of an estate, it is your responsibility to honor the wishes of the deceased. Your first task is to locate and identify those items designated in the will that are to be distributed to family, friends, or institutions.

TIP Do not hire anyone who offers to lowball values to save the estate money.

Prior to distribution, these items need to be valued. Their value is part of the estate. Unless you possess the expert skills required, hire a professional to determine these values, as discussed in chapter three. Make it clear that the valuation report has to be based on fair market value. Once the valuation is done, encourage the recipients to make arrangements to pick up and move their objects.

As executor you need to decide if the estate will be responsible for paying to move objects designated in the will to the location of the recipient. Consult with your attorney on proper procedure. In most cases transfer of title occurs at the point where the objects are located. Moving from this location to another is the responsibility of the recipient.

The waters are muddied from this point forward. If the deceased attached a list of distribution wishes to the will rather than specifically designating these wishes in the will, the executor may be in a position to decide whether or not to honor them. Again check with your attorney to determine the laws of the state in which the estate is probated. If bound by the wishes of that list, the executor needs to locate these objects and treat them as set out above. If not the executor has tough decisions to make as to which wishes, if any, will be followed. If moneys are needed to settle the estate, the executor may choose to sell these items rather than distribute them.

You may find that the deceased has placed stickers with people's names on the bottom of objects. The implication is that the owner wanted these individuals to have these objects. These stickers have no legal validity unless specified in the will. Whether or not these objects go to the individuals named rests solely in the discretion of the executor. Again financial and other estate considerations will play a role in whether or not these wishes are honored.

FACT People often promise other people objects on the spur of the moment or with a true intention to do so, but never record these promises in writing.

A Personal Story

Paul Llewellyn Rinker, my father, and Richard Paul Rinker, my brother and only sibling, died in 1966. Josephine Prosser Rinker, my mother, died in 1977. My nuclear family was very close. My mother and I maintained close contact with my Rinker aunts and uncles and cousins following my father's and brother's deaths.

My mother's final six months were difficult ones. I was assisted by several of my Prosser aunts in caring for my mother during her last three months.

I was my mother's sole heir and executor of her will. I inherited everything my mother owned.

Knowing that my mother's will did not contain any gifts of personal property to anyone other than me, I asked my mother to help me draw up a list of things she owned that she had promised to others. My mother agreed. We reviewed the list several times in the two months prior to her death.

Although I never promised my mother to honor her wishes to the letter, I had every intention of doing so. There was nothing on the list that I wanted.

Mother died. A memorial service was held. Family came from far and wide. My mother was well liked.

A day after the funeral, two of my father's sisters came to my family home for a visit. After some niceties, one aunt said, "We are here to pick up the chairs your mother promised us." My mother owned a pair of balloon back Rococo Revival chairs that she had refinished and reupholstered.

At first my aunts failed to notice the look of surprise on my face. There was no Rococo Revival chair promised to either aunt on the list my mother and I had compiled.

When I explained that I had such a list and it was prepared by mother and me, my aunt replied, "It does not make any difference. Your mother promised us each a chair, and we want them."

A problem with dealing with aunts and uncles is that they never accept your evolution into adulthood. They always assume a position of authority and command based solely on the fact that they are a generation older than you.

Fortunately this occurred in 1977 and not today when I am older, wiser, and more defiant. To preserve family harmony and peace, it seemed easier at the time to give each aunt a chair, so I did.

THE REST OF THE STORY: Both aunts have died. Each aunt had two children. The chair given to my first aunt has disappeared. Neither of the children have it. The second chair is currently in the possession of a cousin. Knowing its meaning to me, she has offered to return it.

Normally individuals appointed as executors know about their role in advance. Whenever possible the executor should sit down with the individual whose estate he will be managing and discuss any promises made concerning personal or other property. Take detailed notes.

This instructions/wish list should be reviewed once a year. People can and do change their minds. Whenever discussing the list, the potential executor needs to make it clear to the owner that these are instructions/wishes only and unless they are also specified in the will they are not enforceable under the law.

For downsizers, you are going to encounter objects that you would like to pass on to family and friends rather than keep or sell. These are your Pile 2. As a downsizer, you are in a bonus situation.

You are able to ask these individuals if they want and will treasure your gift. Hopefully, they will answer honestly. If they answer yes, be pleased. If they answer no, you can offer the object to someone else or place it in your sale pile.

Pile 3: Objects Requested by Heirs, Family, Friends, and Others

Assuming the estate has more than enough liquid capital to pay all the inheritance taxes or the person downsizing has more than they can take, the opportunity exists to honor requests from heirs, family, friends, and others. The question is: Where do you draw the line? The answer is heirs first, family second, friends third, and then the others.

TIP Never say to anyone, "take anything you like." You might be surprised. They might like everything and want to take it all.

When allowing any individual to express an interest in an object, you need to make it very clear that accepting their expression of interest is not tantamount to gifting the object to them. Caught up in the spirit of the moment, many individuals fail to hear the phrase "I'll take it under advisement." Even if you shout it or hand it to them in writing, they can miss it.

Initially limit the number of items an individual can request—ten to fifteen for each heir, two to three for each additional family member, and one or two for everyone else. You can always expand the list later.

If asked to express an interest in an object or objects, the person expressing the interest is likely to assume that the object will be gifted to him. Simply put, he will not expect to pay for it. If this is not your intention, you need to make this clear from the beginning.

⚱ FACT Nowhere does it say you have to pass down objects for free.

Some individuals avoid this problem by telling everyone, children, grandchildren, etc., that they plan to sell everything they themselves do not want. If an heir, family member, friend, or other individual wants an item he or she can buy it. This approach is justified based on its ability to avoid making a painful decision of who gets what if more than one individual expresses an interest in an object. All it really does is favor the individuals with the deepest pockets.

Think twice before following this procedure. I have watched family members destroy each other in bidding wars at auctions in an attempt to keep a treasured heirloom.

⚱ FACT Family things should remain in the family as long as there are family members who will care for them.

Do not for one minute hesitate to ask an individual why he wants an object or how he plans to use it. You have every right to question the motivation behind his request. If you gift an object, you deserve to know how it is going to be used. If you are not satisfied with the proposed use, then do not gift it. If you sell the object, you relinquish all rights to control its use. In fact, whether you gift or sell an object, title transfers at the moment of gift or sale. All bets and promises are cancelled.

At this point in the dispersal process, your goal is merely to create piles. The selection of the method or methods to dispose of these piles is discussed in subsequent chapters.

Piles one through three involve objects set aside to be kept. The next three piles focus on identifying objects to sell or donate. You are done identifying objects you want to keep.

Pile 4: Antiques, Fine Art Objects, and Collectibles

Antiques, fine art, and collectibles are classified as appreciating personal property. What is critical is that these objects have a secondary retail market value above their reuse value, an intrinsic worth determined by a collector and/or decorator.

You are going to divide these items into four piles—high-end, middle market, common, and primarily decorator value. This will assist you in selecting the most effective method of sale.

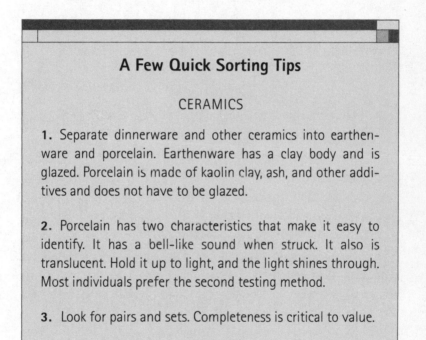

A Few Quick Sorting Tips

CERAMICS

1. Separate dinnerware and other ceramics into earthenware and porcelain. Earthenware has a clay body and is glazed. Porcelain is made of kaolin clay, ash, and other additives and does not have to be glazed.

2. Porcelain has two characteristics that make it easy to identify. It has a bell-like sound when struck. It also is translucent. Hold it up to light, and the light shines through. Most individuals prefer the second testing method.

3. Look for pairs and sets. Completeness is critical to value.

JEWELRY

1. Separate jewelry into pieces containing precious and semiprecious stones and those that do not.

2. Most pieces containing precious stones will have mounts made of gold, platinum, or silver. In America the use of precious metal markings was not common until the twentieth century. Test all Victorian-era and early-twentieth-century pieces.

3. Separate costume jewelry into four piles: (1) marked pieces, (2) pieces with sterling silver mounts, (3) sets, for example, a bracelet with matching earrings and/or pin, and (4) the rest.

4. Figural pins from Christmas trees to animals are popular. Put them aside.

Christie Romero's *Warman's Jewelry*, published by KP Books, an imprint of F+W Books, is an excellent reference source.

SILVER

1. Divide silver into two piles: (1) silver plate and (2) sterling. Even if a sterling piece, which is 925 parts silver per thousand, has no collector value, it has melt value.

2. The 925 sterling standard is used by the United States and the United Kingdom and its Commonwealth countries. Other countries use different standards. If you find a piece marked 800, 840, or 850, put it on the sterling pile.

3. If the piece is American-made and dates after 1900, if it is not marked STERLING or 925, chances are it is plated.

4. In the nineteenth century the standard was coin silver, which varies from 750 to 900 parts silver per thousand. Unmarked older silver may in fact be coin silver. If you aren't sure how old a piece is, don't rush to put it in the silver plate pile—first take it to an expert.

The first three piles are based on collector value. Objects selected to be placed in these piles should fall into well-established collecting categories. The ideal object is one that has the ability to appeal to collectors in two or more collecting categories.

Reserve your fourth pile for antiques, fine art objects, and collectibles whose decorative, conversation, and/or nostalgia appeal exceeds their collecting worth. This will or should be the smallest of the four piles.

Pile 4A is comprised of those antiques, fine art objects, and collectibles that have a potential sale value to you of five hundred dollars or more. "Potential sale value" to you is the key phrase. This is a wholesale, not a retail, value.

FACT The only value in which you are interested is what you can obtain for an object, not what a dealer or auctioneer can expect.

If you do not have the skill to identify the objects that belong in this pile, hire professional help. If you suspect you have a large number of objects that belong in this group, you already have hired an appraiser to do a walk-through appraisal. The walk-through appraisal should have identified ninety-five-plus percent of these objects.

If a significant number of questions arise, you may wish to consider bringing the appraiser back for another consultation. Most appraisers leave their business card and encourage clients to call with questions. If the questions are minimal, often no charge is assessed.

Pile 4B is comprised of those antiques, fine art objects, and collectibles whose potential resale value to you is between one hundred and five hundred dollars. Items in this pile are likely to date from the post-1945 period or be comprised of stand-alone smalls.

FACT A major mistake individuals make is assuming that an object has little to no secondary market value because they grew up with it.

Do not be surprised when this pile is completed that it contains a large number of items you had as a child or purchased as a young adult. The hot collecting decades at the moment are the 1960s and 1970s, not the 1860s and 1870s. Today's young buyers are much more "me" focused. They have more interest in their own things and those of their parents than they do the objects that belonged to their grandparents or great-grandparents.

Pile 4C is comprised of those antiques, fine art objects, and collectibles whose potential sale value to you is between twenty and one hundred dollars. While the largest of the three piles, it most likely will produce the smallest amount of income. However there is power in numbers. One hundred objects that average thirty dollars each when sold produce three thousand dollars.

TIP If an object is older than fifty years of age, consider placing it in Pile 4C.

It is better to put too many things in this pile during the first sort than too few. When the initial sorting is completed, this is the first pile that gets a second look.

Pile 4D includes objects whose principal decorative, conversational, or nostalgic value exceeds their collecting value. Be highly selective when creating this pile. There needs to be universal agreement among everyone asked that these objects achieve the goal set for them.

The objects in this pile should be big and showy. They must stand out. Be the center of attention. They must speak period or cause the viewer to automatically ask, "What is that?"

As you create each of these four piles, keep a running total of the objects found in each pile. Even if the number is off by a few, it still will be helpful when considering sale methods.

Pile 5: Reusables

A reusable is an object whose principal value is reuse for the purpose for which the object was manufactured. Simply put, it is too good to throw out.

Several quick rules will help you identify these objects:

1) Is the object less than ten years old?
2) Is the object something individuals use every day?
3) If I did not have one, needed one, and could buy one for ten cents on the dollar or less, would I do it?
4) Does the object look relatively new?

Divide your reusables into two piles—the first consisting of like-new objects and the second consisting of moderately to heavily used objects. Value rests in the first pile, but there are buyers for the objects in the second. Objects that are incomplete, broken, and heavily battered belong in Pile 7.

Divide objects by type the minute you start creating piles. Just because these objects will not produce the same level of income you will get from the sale of antiques, fine art objects, and collectibles, does not mean that you should treat them disrespectfully. Place them in the boxes carefully. Avoid breaking them.

Focus on creating sets and complete units. Americans think in even numbers. If you find you have a complete dinnerware service for seven, call it "service for six" and note that you are including extra pieces. The same applies to glassware, flatware, and any other objects sold in groups. When selling always insist the purchaser buy the full set. Avoid selling individual pieces unless you absolutely have to do it.

All pots need lids. All electrical appliances need their cords. All

Dividing Reuseables into Types of Goods

Create boxes for each of the following categories. When a box is full, pack the objects, seal the box, and mark it.

Accessories

Appliances

Baby items

Books

Ceramics

Clothing, adult

Clothing, children

Decorative items

Dinnerware

Glass

Jewelry

Kitchen accessories and utensils

Lawn equipment

Office equipment and supplies

Sporting equipment

Tabletop items

Tools

Toys

Textiles

Note 1: Include clothing accessories in the clothing categories.

Note 2: Add boxes for other categories as needed.

blenders need their accessories. You get the idea. A unit has to be complete if you want to obtain the best price for it.

Put the oddball, mismatched objects in an oddball box. Even if these items only sell for a nickel or dime, you are ahead financially. Do not waste your time trying to decide what potential customers want. Let them decide. Give customers plenty of choice.

Pile 6: Objects for Donation

Besides doing a good deed, you can make money by donating objects to charitable groups. When downsizing or settling an estate, most individuals focus primarily on clothing. This is an extremely narrow approach.

FACT The vintage clothing market is very strong. Those clothes you are thinking of donating may have value to a collector.

Before you start piling all the unwanted clothing in bags to take to charity, take a few minutes and examine the clothing. If the clothing has designer labels or speaks period, that is, represents the dominant design styles of an era, it should be sold rather than donated. Vintage clothing collectors also love accessories, for example, hats, purses, and shoes. Set aside all clothing accessories that were once trendy. Finally many individuals store clothing in the boxes they were in when they purchased them. Often these boxes are from department stores that are no longer in existence. Hatbox collectors eagerly seek examples from the 1920s through the 1970s.

The secondary retail market for contemporary upholstered furniture, bedding, and inexpensive furnishings purchased new from large chain stores is minimal to nonexistent. If you live in a large- to medium-size city, chances are there are organizations that welcome such items for distribution to low-income families.

TIP Develop an "if you cannot sell it, donate it" attitude. Toss an object only as a last resort.

When you look in the kitchen cupboard and pantry, you are going to find large quantities of food that you bought with the intention to use but never did. Some will have spoiled or the recommended use date will be long expired. Toss these items along with those products which have been opened. Donate the remainder. Most communities have food bank programs. They welcome donations. Just because you never used it does not mean others will not.

Consider donating all books and records whose secondary retail value is under five dollars, probably ninety-five-plus percent of the books and records encountered, to the local library or American Association of University Women's book sale. Most will be purchased for reuse.

TIP If you encounter a private library with a quantity of leather-bound volumes, historical titles, or art books, hire the services of a book appraiser.

Chapter twelve explains how to value these donations. Whether included as part of the estate or claimed individually, these donations are money in the bank.

Pile 7: To Toss or Not to Toss

Before you toss any object, consider its potential scrap value. Metals, textiles, and paper all have scrap value that can produce income. Glass and plastic have recyclable value. It never hurts to be a good citizen.

Scrap

We live in a throwaway economy. We no longer expect things to last a lifetime. We trash rather than recycle. Most individuals under the age of forty have never been to a scrap yard.

Jason Goldberg, my stepson, heads a demolition company. Much of his income comes from selling industrial scrap. I never cease to be amazed at what he sells and for how much he sells it.

When downsizing or cleaning out a house, think in terms of three types of scrap—paper, textiles, and metal. Paper is purchased by the pound. Most individuals think of paper in terms of newsprint. Paper also means books and magazines. If it is made of paper, consider scrapping it before throwing it out.

Divide textiles into natural and synthetics. Natural textiles, for example, cotton and wool, can be sold for scrap. This material is recycled. Most table linens have scrap value.

Copper is the hot metal of the moment. Many pots and plans have copper bottoms. In order to get the copper value, you will have to cut the copper bottoms off the pans. Brass, cast iron, and steel are other metals of interest to a scrap dealer. When you take mixed metals to a scrap yard, you get the lowest metal's value for the lot. You maximize your return when you separate metals by type.

There are recycling centers that buy crushed aluminum cans and other products made from aluminum. Once again there are different values for different types of aluminum. Separate aluminum cans from scrap aluminum such as lawn chair frames, old siding, etc. Also many recycling centers prefer that you do not crush the cans. Their crushing/cubing machines work more efficiently with uncrushed cans.

Recyclable Goods

Alas the only value in plastic is the ability to recycle it. The same is true for glass. Many communities require you to divide your trash into recyclable groups. Even if you live in or are settling an estate in an area where this is not the case, consider being a good citizen by culling out the recyclables and taking them to a recycling center.

Landfill

Send damaged and broken items, food that is no longer usable, food that has been opened, and heavily worn items to the landfill. Bag and put this material out for trash pickup as you go through the sorting process.

TIP Trust your instincts. You are smart enough to recognize junk when you see it.

Downsizing and settling an estate are not the time to get caught up in the wish that someone will buy a heavily damaged object for the parts or will take it home and restore it. Buyers walk away from incomplete objects. Few have the time to do restoration work.

Be merciful. If an object's functionality has been lost, end its life. If it cannot be scrapped, toss it.

A Caveat: Personal Papers

Americans are savers. They save everything from cancelled personal checks to copies of paid bills. Personal information needs to be destroyed.

If you are going to toss it, run it through a paper shredder. If your local ordinances allow, consider burning. No matter the method you select, make certain it is destroyed.

I collect credit cards. Friends often offer me old credit cards. Before accepting, I ask a simple question, "Did you cancel the account?" If they answer, "No, I just received a new credit card and thought you would like the old one," I point out that they have just given me access to their credit card account number.

If downsizing you should take your financial and tax records for the last five years with you to your new home. Destroy the older records. If you are the executor of an estate, one of the first steps you need to take is to cancel all existing charge accounts. Once done, turn your attention to destroying the old records.

In Summary

Now that you have your objects in piles, take a day or two to review what you have done. Refine the selection process.

Now it is time to think about disposing of the piles. The remaining chapters in *Sell, Keep, or Toss?* explore the selling and other disposal options available to you.

CHAPTER FIVE

Disposing of a Collection(s)

WHAT percent of Americans collect? Studies commissioned by eBay indicate that the answer is just over half the country's population, but based on my field observations and conversations with individuals in and out of the antiques and collectibles field, the number may be as high as seventy-five percent or more. America is a nation of collectors.

When someone says, "I do not collect," I respond, "Do you own ten or more of any object that you have not used in the last two years? What about shoes?" America is home to millions of closet shoe collectors. They just do not know they are collectors.

Kidding aside, the disposal of collections that include antiques, collectibles, desirables, and fine arts require a different approach than that used for the disposal of family heirlooms and household goods. This process requires expertise, and if you do not have it, it will be worth hiring someone who does.

Most of the information in this chapter will apply to those charged with the task of disposing of a significant collection. If you do not need to perform this task, feel free to skip ahead.

FACT Most individuals do not have one collection. They have several.

It is a rare individual who only has one major collection. Most collectors have a half dozen or more collections, each separate and unrelated to the other. Each collection can have dozens of subcollections within it. What makes perfect sense to the collector may represent utter confusion to the uninitiated.

TIP Just because a collection is small does not mean it cannot be extremely valuable.

Collections vary in size from a few dozen objects to thousands of pieces. The value of the individual objects, not the size of the collections, is the key to understanding them for disposal purposes.

When Fox's *Personal FX* television show was on the air, a representative of the show called a major Coca-Cola collector to inquire about featuring a visit to his collection on the show. The representative asked the collector, "How many objects do you have in your collection?" "Around fifty," the collector responded. "I'm sorry. You do not have enough," the representative replied and hung up. I saw this collection. Although small, it contained the top fifty Coca-Cola items. The collection's value was in the hundreds of thousands of dollars.

Collectors tend to keep matters relating to their collections to themselves. Often they don't want their spouses to know what they have paid for their pieces. For many people, collecting is private, personal, and emotional. Collectors have a difficult time explaining why they did what they did, and don't want to be called upon to justify their purchases.

Few collections are assembled by couples. If a spouse collects, it is usually something diametrically opposed to what the other spouse collects. Collectors also are loath to share information with their heirs or executor.

The thought of selling a collection or portion of a collection is abhorrent to a collector. Investors buy and sell antiques, collectibles, fine arts, and desirables for profit. They are not in collecting for love as are collectors. All investors care about is the money.

Collectors buy objects planning to keep them until they die or some catastrophic need arises where they have no choice but to sell. As a result collectors do not view their collections as monetary assets. Collections are things that give them pleasure. In collectors' minds, once they have spent the money to acquire an object, this money is gone from their life forever.

Thanks to this collector mind-set, the person or persons faced with the disposal of a collector's collections face a heavy burden. What follows is designed to ease that burden.

What Constitutes a Collection

There always is more to a collection than is visible to the eye. Typically a collector displays one-half to two-thirds of his collection. The balance is in storage. You need to find it all before deciding how to dispose of it.

In addition a collection is more than the objects that comprise it. Most collectors have an extensive research library consisting of reference books, specialized periodicals, auction catalogs, clippings from magazines and papers, etc., an ephemera collection ranging from manufacturer's sale catalogs to advertising memorabilia, boxes and packaging, and repair parts. All these items have value.

FACT Rarely is a collection housed only in one room.

Collections quickly exceed the space the collector initially allotted to them. Although the bulk of the collection may be displayed or stored in a single room, check the collector's den, office, basement, attic, closets, and garage. You will find objects and other material related to the collection stored in these areas as well.

Collection Checklist

Use the following checklist when searching for items that constitute a collection:

OBJECTS

Single objects (keep duplicates together)
Boxed in their period packaging
Collector editions
Prototypes (manufacturers' models)
Spare parts

ACQUISITION/PURCHASE RECORDS

Address book or file   **Photographs of collection**
Display or loan history   **Sales receipts**

ADVERTISING OF ALL TYPES

Magazine tear sheets   **Store displays**

REFERENCE MATERIALS

Auction catalogs   **Price guides, general**
Clipping files   **Price guides, specific**
Collector's club material   **Reference books**
  Membership list   **Trade periodicals and**
  Newsletters   **newspapers**
Manufacturers' material
  Brochures
  Catalogs
  Letterheads

You need to bring these scattered parts into a common area before making any dispersal decisions. If you are not certain whether or not an item belongs in the collection, decide in favor of yes. Let an expert cull it out.

Learning About the Collections

Before contacting anyone or accepting any offer of help in respect to disposing of a collection or collections, you need to do a quick study and learn at least a little about the objects with which you will be dealing. Ideally the collector has an extensive reference library. Pick one or two general reference texts and read them. If the collector was a member of one or more collectors' clubs, take time to scan the club's newsletter.

FACT Overvaluing the potential worth of a collection is one of the biggest mistakes an individual who is unfamiliar with a collection makes.

If the reference books you decide to read are price guides, remember that the prices in these guides are retail, not wholesale prices. These prices can cloud your judgment. Take time for an immediate reality check. Research the value of several of the objects in the collection on eBay. Compare eBay auction results with the price guide values.

The collector may have insisted many times over the years that the collection is worth a lot. Keep in mind that "worth" is a relative term. The collector may have been talking about emotional and not monetary worth, or the market for these collectibles may have changed drastically in the time since the collection was assembled. "A lot" also is open to interpretation. Be prepared to find that the collection may be less valuable than you had hoped.

◆ | FACT The worth of a collection is the amount for which you can sell it—nothing more, nothing less.

The adage "a little knowledge is a dangerous thing" does not apply in this instance. Knowledge, even a little, is your best friend. The knowledge you gain is critical to your evaluating the truthfulness of the information you will be given by experts, fellow collectors, and friends.

Getting the Right Help

If you have made the difficult and painful decision as a collector to dispose of your collections, do not base your disposal decisions solely on your knowledge. Unless you have been actively buying, selling, and tracking the collecting categories for the past five years, consider hiring an expert who is far more familiar with the current secondary resale market to do an evaluation of the marketing potential of your collections.

An independent appraiser familiar with the collecting category is an excellent first choice. An advanced collector is a second option, albeit ask first if there are objects in the collection that he might wish to buy. If he answers yes, then continue your search. There is a growing number of individuals specializing in the disposal of collections. Few advertise. Most rely primarily on referrals. If such a person exists in your community, changes are he or she is know to the local estate attorneys and historical organizations. You find such a person by asking.

Collectors tend to cut back on their collecting in their early sixties. Unless a health or other issue develops, they do not think about selling their collections until their mid- to late seventies. This means they have been out of the market for ten years or longer. In today's trendy antiques and collectibles market, two years is a long time. Ten years is a lifetime.

◆ | FACT Most collections assembled in the 1930s through the 1950s are declining rather than gaining in value.

Collectors have memory problems. First, they remember what they paid for things. They consider any price lower than this amount as a personal affront. Second, they believe everything they read at any point in time that states their objects are worth more than they paid for them. Collectors have a "highest price possible" mentality.

Whether you are a collector who is disposing of his collection with a warm hand or an executor faced with a myriad of collections about which he knows very little, hire an expert to evaluate the collection. Besides being market knowledgeable, the expert has to be client focused. His only interest must be the client who hired him. This means that the expert cannot buy any object or item in the collections. The expert will be expected to recommend and evaluate disposal options. Hence the expert should not be an employee of an auction firm, a dealer, or a fellow collector. All efforts must be made to avoid conflicts of interest.

Personally interview any individual you are considering hiring. Ask for a list of his credentials in advance. Probe his availability and openly discuss his fee structure. Most important, hire a person whom you can trust.

◆ | TIP An astute collector aids his executor by including in his will specific instructions about whom to contact to assist in the dispersal of his collections.

Be leery of offers of help from the following sources—fellow collectors, specialized auction house personnel, and well-meaning friends. The first two groups will play an important role later, when you are exploring sale options. No matter how well-meaning friends may be, chances are they do not have the expertise you need. Thanks, but no thanks!

Where Is the Value?

Half or more of the value of any collection rests in the top fifteen to twenty percent of the items in the collection. Stated another way, the majority of the value is in the high-end pieces. High-end pieces are known as ultimate (masterpiece) units and upper-echelon pieces.

Dividing the collection into high- , middle-, and low-end components is a primary reason why you need to hire an expert. The expert knows how to tell the difference. Chances are that you do not.

Condition is critical to value. Grading antiques, collectibles, fine arts, and desirables is a critical skill and highly subjective. The expert you hire must have grading as well as identification and market knowledge skills.

Not all high-end value is in the objects. The value of some secondary material, for example, advertising display pieces or period boxes, may exceed the value of most objects in the collection. Some trade catalogs command prices in the hundreds of dollars. Your expert has to have the ability to separate the wheat from the chaff.

TIP Do not allow anyone to cherry-pick a collection.

Individuals do not collect in isolation. While the collector may not have been an active member of a collectors' club, he certainly made friends along the way. These friends know and are familiar with his collection. They know the objects and other items the collection contains and those that are not found in their collection. They covet.

The minute word hits the collecting community that a collection is for sale, fellow, or perhaps a better term is *rival,* collectors come out of the woodwork. At no previous point in life did the collector have as many friends as he does now.

All these friends have one goal in mind. They want to get inside and acquire the pieces they desire before knowledge about the sale of the collection becomes too widespread. The one thing they do not want to do is buy the entire collection, unless they can acquire it for pennies on the dollar. What they really want is to cherry-pick the collection, that is, buy what they want, usually the high-end pieces, at a greatly reduced price and leave the common material for someone else.

There is only one way to deal with these individuals. Tell them NO! No one gets a peek until the final decision is made as to how the collection will be dispersed.

Collectors' Clubs

Today's collectors are organized. Collectors' clubs exist for hundreds of collecting categories. The ideal situation is finding that there are one or more collectors' clubs whose focus is the collection or collections you are responsible for selling.

The One Book You Need

If you are only going to buy one book to assist you in disposing of your collection, the book you need is:

David J. Maloney Jr., *Maloney's Antiques & Collectibles Resource Directory, Sixth Edition*, published by Krause Books (KP Books), an imprint of F+W Publications.

Maloney's contains information about auction services, appraisers, clubs and associations, collectors, experts, museums and libraries, periodicals, restoration services, supplies, and a host of other data for over three thousand antiques and collectibles collecting categories.

The information found in *Maloney's* is available online at *www.maloneysonline.com.*

Collectors' club membership includes the majority of the key collectors in any given collecting category. Because of the strong sense of rivalry in collecting, there are some very independent-minded collectors who want nothing to do with joining a collectors' club. Since they prefer to be out of sight, put them out of your mind. Focus on the collectors you can access quickly and easily.

Collectors' clubs offer a wide range of services from monthly or quarterly newsletters to hosting annual conventions. Many newsletters allow classified and display advertisements. When you are ready to sell, this is a great way to reach potential customers or spread the word about a major auction or sale. Some annual conventions feature an "auction" night. If this is the case, you may want to consider arranging to sell the collection at the annual convention auction or a day or two prior to the convention at an auction house located in the convention city.

FACT The Web site *www.collectors.org*, home of the National Association of Collectors and National Association of Collecting Clubs, is well worth a visit.

Many collectors' clubs publish their membership list. Annual dues rarely exceed fifty dollars. If you do not belong to a collectors' club or if the person whose collection you are selling did not belong to a collectors' club, join immediately if there is a club associated with that collecting category. Fifty dollars or less is a very cheap price to pay for a list that contains the names, addresses, phone numbers, and e-mail addresses of hundreds of potential buyers.

Donating a Collection

When a collection is sold, it is gone. Many collectors simply refuse to face this eventuality. Hence they leave the dispersal of their collections to their surviving spouse, heir, or executor.

Many collectors dream of their collection surviving intact and on display in a museum. If the surviving spouse has ample funds and does not need the money the sale of a collection represents or the collection represents only a small portion of the estate, the surviving spouse or executor often will explore donating the deceased's collection to a museum or historical society in his or her memory. The dream is always the same—a separate room in which the collection is displayed much as it was at the collectors' home and a plaque and other signage acknowledging the collector.

Dreams are one thing, reality another. Today's museums no longer accept collections just because they are offered. A museum acquisition committee reviews the proposed gift and decides whether or not the collection fits into the museum's mission statement.

TIP Before donating your collection to a museum, visit the museum. Check issues such as the museum's humidity and temperature control system, storage areas, and security.

The more conditions attached to a donation, the less likely the museum is to accept it. Demands that collection be housed in a separate room or gallery, always be on display, the display never changed, no object or part of the collection sold, and objects never allowed to leave the museum on loan usually result in a quick refusal. Museums have learned from past experience that the best gift is one that comes with no restrictions. Once title is transferred to the museum, the museum is free to do with it what it wants. This freedom may and often does result in selling off parts of the collection the museum acquisition board considers unnecessary to fulfilling the museum's mission.

Much to the surprise of potential donors, the museum may refuse to accept the gift of the collection without a significant monetary contribution to pay for the installation and long-term maintenance of the collection. Many of today's museums are property and collection rich and operational capital poor.

If a museum does agree to accept a collection with stipulations attached, consider appointing a committee of two or three individuals who have the right to visit the museum every five years to make certain the terms of the gift are being followed. The gift agreement should clearly empower the committee to remove the collection if they feel the terms of the gift are not being fulfilled.

FACT Collectors love the objects in their collection. Museums simply care for them.

I worked in the museum field for nearly fifteen years at the beginning of my professional career. I saw firsthand how museums treat collections, especially those with conditions attached. The simple truth is that as members of the professional staff and governing board change, the knowledge of what those conditions are and the willingness to abide by them become distant memories, memories so distant that they are forgotten. I have no intention of donating anything I own to a museum. Enough said!

Keeping a Few Memories

Should a spouse or heirs keep a few pieces from a collection as a remembrance of the collector? The answer is NO.

FACT The sale of a collection creates a sense of excitement. Any suggestion that some pieces have been held back greatly dampens that enthusiasm.

The reason is twofold. First, the pieces selected are often the best pieces in the collection. Removing these pieces from the collection is "cherry-picking" in another guise. A collection's sales appeal rests primarily on the top pieces in the collection. Remove them and the general impression of the collection's value is significantly lowered.

If you must keep a few pieces in remembrance of the collector, select a few of the most common pieces or duplicate pieces. When selecting a duplicate piece, leave the example in the best condition grade in the collection.

Resist the temptation of holding back based on the premise that since I do not need the money now, I will sell the objects when I do. You already have learned that the antiques and collectibles market is trendy. Some values do increase over time. Equally true, some values fall.

Passing the Torch

The argument often is made that a collector never really owns an object. He is merely its custodian until the time comes to pass it along to the next owner. It is a valid argument.

While there are always exceptions, collectors take better care of the objects in their collection than do many historical societies and museums. If every collector donated his collection to a museum or other public instruction, what would future collectors have to collect?

Once a decision has been made to sell a collection, there are two basic choices—sell the collection as a single unit or break it apart. While the first approach saves time, the second approach maximizes the return.

Single Buyer

Until the last two decades of the twentieth century, the assumption in the antiques and collectibles community was that a collection's value was enhanced if sold as a unit. An appraiser valued the individual pieces and a twenty- to thirty-percent premium was added. The premium was a value assigned to the time and expenses the buyer would save assuming he had to assemble the collection from scratch. It makes sense, especially if you are the seller.

This is no longer true in the twenty-first century. Today a buyer of a complete collection expects to buy at a twenty-five to forty percent discount. The assumptions are the buyer is (1) saving the seller the selling costs of disposing of the collection and (2) taking everything, even the items he does not want or duplicate examples already in his collection. This makes sense, especially if you are the buyer.

FACT The burden of what to ask for a collection rests on the seller. The buyer's responsibility is to say yes, no, or make a counteroffer.

Before offering a collection for private sale, make certain you have three or four strong potential buyers. If a collection is offered for sale and does not sell, its value is tainted. Collectors will ask, "Why did it not sell? What did the potential buyers see in the collection that caused them to walk away?"

Setting a price and offering the collection for that amount is one dispersal method. If selecting this method, bring in your strongest buyer first.

Negotiating is a standard buying practice in the antiques, fine arts, and collectibles fields. Resist the temptation to add a ten- to twenty-percent premium to what you are expecting so that when you finally negotiate, the price you settle upon is the one that you wanted in the first place. Experienced buyers see through this immediately.

TIP The closer you set your price to full market value, the more difficult it will be to obtain it. Think twenty to twenty-five percent less.

Set a price and stand firm. If the buyer fails to meet it and counter-offers, explain that you have scheduled to show the collection to others, and, if nothing develops from these potential buyers, you will consider his offer. Experienced buyers know to try the "my offer is only good now" purchasing strategy. They are fully aware that it is hard to walk away from money in hand. You have to find the strength to remain firm to your sales plan. If you and your adviser have confidence that the price you are asking is well within market parameters, then you have nothing to lose by moving forward. Further many buyers will back off the now-or-never approach when faced with possibly losing the purchase.

Another sales approach is the best bid sales method. Give each potential buyer who inspects the collection a blank card and an envelope. Set a minimum bid. Tell the potential buyer to place his bid in the envelope. When the last potential buyer inspects the collection, you will open the envelope and sell the collection to the highest bidder.

FACT Tell bidders that they should not bid more than they are willing to pay.

Do not be surprised if these potential buyers ask you to accept a selling approach that adjusts the winning bid to one standard auction bid jump above the second highest bid. Refuse to do this.

Also refuse to negotiate with the winning bidder. He named his price. He must be prepared to honor it.

Dealer

One or two dealers often play a key role in creating a collection. Some collectors feel strongly that when it comes time to dispose of their collections, the primary dealer from whom they purchased the collection should be the individual responsible for disposing of it.

Most antiques and collectibles dealers do not have the funds to purchase a collection outright. Just like today's business community, antiques and collectibles dealers maintain a greatly reduced inventory. No one can afford to be inventory rich.

When a dealer is offered a collection for sale, he usually insists on a consignment arrangement. Such an arrangement is very risky.

FACT Never agree to allow anything to be sold on consignment without a contract.

It may take the dealer years to sell everything in the collection. In fact, the dealer may never sell many of the common pieces. It is a major challenge keeping track of what is and is not sold. Most dealers prefer not to report more than quarterly. Issues such as who is responsible for loss, theft, and security while the collection is in the possession of the dealer, percentage of payment (a flat percentage versus a floating percentage based on final sales price), and return of unsold merchandise at the end of the consignment contract also cloud the sales process.

If you are willing to devote the time and diligence to making the consignment process work, then proceed. If you are looking for a fast exit from the collection, this is not the choice for you.

Auction

A single-owner auction catalog documents a collection. It is an ideal method for a collector or executor to provide a permanent record of the collector's accomplishment to heir, family, friends, etc. Even if the collection is too small for a single-owner sale, its inclusion as a unit in the catalog of a larger sale achieves the same goal. Obviously the cost of the catalog has to be borne by someone. The collector always expects the auctioneer to pay for it out of his share of the sale proceeds. Typically the cost is shared.

FACT Auctioneers need to group some objects in lots in order to sell them effectively.

Collectors love every single piece in their collection. Little wonder they expect an auctioneer to sell each piece separately. This expectation is totally unrealistic.

Most auctioneers have a minimum price per lot they wish to achieve. The amount varies depending on whether the auctioneer is selling box lots or a cataloged listing. However, whether box lot or catalog listing, objects often need to be grouped to achieve the auctioneer's goal.

Since chapter seven is devoted to how to find the right auctioneer and what to expect in the way of services, there is no need to duplicate this information here. If you are only dealing with the disposal of a collection, you may want to jump to chapter seven and read it now.

If a collection or collections is only one of the dispersal issues with which you are dealing, read on.

CHAPTER SIX

Dealing with Family and Friends

E VERYONE wants a piece of the action. This truism definitely applies when disposing of an estate or downsizing. Those responsible for the dispersal never knew they had so many good friends or that the deceased was so widely love and respected.

FACT Face the fact that you will not please everyone and in fact may make some enemies.

The best executor is a person who is thick-skinned, that is, capable of letting criticism roll off his back and not take it personally. The same is true for the person or persons involved in downsizing. Everybody thinks they know how to do the job you are facing better than you. Maybe they do. Maybe they do not. It does not matter. They are not in charge. You are.

If your goal is to keep everyone friends and avoid controversy, you will never get the job done. Friction is inevitable. Your job is to anticipate and control it. If surface calm and happiness prevails at the end, pat yourself on the back. You have done better than most.

Family First

You need to establish a pecking order within the family. This pecking order usually becomes the picking order, that is, who has first, second, third, etc., choice. When an individual does not want to take the responsibility of selecting specific objects for specific individuals, the logical procedure is to ask individuals to indicate the items they would like. This works only if a clearly defined picking order is established.

FACT The right approach is the one you decide to follow.

Standard Pecking Order

Spouse
Children
Grandchildren
Parents
Brothers and sisters
Nieces and nephews
Friends, special (fewer than five in number)
Aunts and uncles
Cousins
Brothers-in-law, sisters-in-law
Grandchildren's spouses
Great-aunts and -uncles
Friends, social
Friends, clubs, organizations, and leagues
Neighbors
Business acquaintances

There is no right approach, although there are plenty of individuals who will argue with you on this. Who comes first, second, or third is your choice. You are not obligated to follow conventional practice. If you want to establish favorites, do not hesitate to do it as long as you are doing it with the full understanding that those not on the favorites list are likely to feel hurt and resentful.

Playing Favorites

There is nothing wrong with playing favorites. We no longer live in a society where the law decrees that property must be inherited by the eldest son. Tradition is not the same as the rule of law. The eldest does not have an inherent right to pick before the youngest, nor does a male have that right over a female. All children do not have to be treated equally. We live in a liberated society. This lifestyle comes with a price tag attached.

The person who is downsizing or acting as executor establishes the rules, providing of course he follows the wishes of the deceased as outlined in the will. It makes sense to ask how a potential recipient has treated the person who is downsizing or the deceased during their lifetime. There is no reason a person who has treated the person downsizing or deceased poorly should inherit equally just because of his or her birthright. On the other hand, you may decide that someone who was particularly helpful to the deceased should pick sooner than their familial relationship would suggest. Our actions are always subject to being weighed and balanced. This is one of those times.

Who Comprises the Next Generation?

Ideally family heirlooms should be passed to the next generation. However before discussing what happens when the family no longer wants the heirlooms of past generations, it is necessary to consider just who constitutes the next generation. In an age of blended families, this is not as easy a question to answer as you might think.

What happens when a man marries a second time, has children from the first but not the second marriage, and dies before the second spouse? If there is no will, the spouse usually inherits a portion of the estate. In many cases the man may leave everything to his present wife because he loves her and because he believes she will do the right thing, whatever that means. Assume the man inherited

Case Study 1

When I was working for the Historical Society of York County in York, Pennsylvania, an elderly woman walked into the society's headquarters one day and offered to donate a large block of historical objects with a York County origin. Her husband, a member of a prominent York County family, had died. This was his second marriage. The gentleman had no children from either marriage. The woman was the legal owner of the objects and had every right to donate them. In fact, she asked that the donation be made in the name of her deceased husband.

The proper gift forms were filled out and signed. The objects represented a major addition to the society's collection.

As it turned out, the brother of the gentleman was a member of the society's board of directors. When he discovered his valued "family" heirlooms were now part of the society's collection, he was furious.

The acquisition committee was pressured by the board member to refuse the donation. They acquiesced. The gift was returned. The brother paid a visit to his brother's widow. You do not have to be a genius to figure out what happened. Badgered and cajoled, the woman reluctantly gave all the "family" heirlooms to the brother.

dozens of family treasures from previous generations. Logic suggests these would go to the children from the first marriage. The law and will may decree otherwise.

This example is just the tip of the iceberg. Other complications include stepchildren, children from multiple marriages, and children who stay with or are loyal to an ex-spouse, or children who are otherwise not traditional "blood heirs." All may feel they have claims. It is the responsibility of the person who is downsizing or acting as executor to determine which claims will be honored and which will not.

The Kids Do Not Want Grandma's China

Downsizing and disposing of an estate are here-and-now situations. The decisions made at this point stand forever. Hindsight is great, but far too late. Do not assume children or grandchildren do not want family heirlooms. Ask them. Hopefully you will be pleasantly surprised.

FACT If you try to predict what your children, family, or friends want, you will be wrong as many times as you are right.

I recently was talking with a couple who were in the process of downsizing. He and his wife set up several tables in the basement and placed on them all the things they did not want but felt their children would. They called their children and agreed on a time when everyone would come and sort through the things. The couple expected the children to fight over some things. Under no circumstances did they expect any objects to remain. At the end of the day, eighty percent of the objects remained on the tables. One child did not take anything from the tables, but spotted an old serving bowl on a shelf. "Can I have that?" he asked. Startled, but pleased that at least he wanted something, the parents said, "Yes." When the father asked his son why he took the bowl, the son replied, "Because I remember it." In this case, it is the memories that made the item valuable to the son.

 **TIP** It is not always about the memories.

Today's young adults are smart. They know that family heirlooms can and often do have a secondary resale value. They may ask for something not because they plan to keep it, but to sell it. If they do not want a treasured family heirloom, it is because the owner failed to create the memory. Do not blame the next generation.

TIP Plead your case.

If a child initially indicates that he has no interest in a family heirloom, consider pleading the case for keeping it in the family. Explain its history and importance. Sharing this helps.

If a child does not want the heirloom, ask the grandchildren. Their memories are different than those of their parents. However also consider the grandchildren's age. If they are not old enough to care for, understand the importance and value of the heirloom, and receive no support from their parents, then seek a home elsewhere.

If the children and grandchildren say no, move down the list of immediate family members—brothers and sisters and nieces and nephews. I own a great many family heirlooms that came from my aunts and uncles simply because my cousins told their parents that they had no interest in them.

Keeping It in the Family

Family heirlooms often play a major role in divorce proceedings. In joint-property states, even if a spouse brought a family heirloom into the marriage, the party seeking the divorce is entitled to half the increase in value the heirloom experienced while the couple was married. If the spouse's parent(s) died, inherited family heirlooms often became jointly owned property. This can make a divorce situation very sticky. As an appraiser I have been involved in both situations and several others, and they are always complicated.

When passing a family heirloom from one generation to another, the person doing so should consider drafting a letter of gift that clearly indicates the gift of the heirloom is made to a specific person. Establish single, not joint, ownership. The goal is to keep the object in the family, independent of what happens in the marriage.

Such an approach does not always sit well with a spouse, especially if the couple has children together. Obviously you need to respect and take these concerns into consideration.

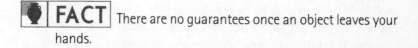 **FACT** There are no guarantees once an object leaves your hands.

What happens if your daughter's husband has a daughter from a previous marriage and they have a son together? When you pass down grandmother's cameo, where is it likely to go? If the son marries and has a daughter, what guarantee do you have that it will go to his daughter and not the stepdaughter or one of her children?

If you have wishes, you need to make them known. If you want control, spell out the conditions and terms in a gift letter or will.

The Selection Process

Distribution of promised items and those specifically designated in the will is finished. It is time to start the selection process that will allow for the disposal of some of the objects that remain.

You have made clear the pecking/picking order. It is time to proceed. Not so fast! You need to establish a few more guidelines and/or rules before the first selection is made.

Rules of the Road

Will selection take place on a one-visit basis or be done by rounds? When children, family, and friends are involved, the standard procedure is the first person picks one object and then the selection passes to the next person. The procedure is repeated until everyone is done picking.

Allowing the first individual to pick everything he wants is unfair to those who follow. Although you as executor or as owner of the items have the right to proceed in this fashion, it is bound to create significant resentment among the other heirs.

How will the picks be valued? Historically the favored approach was one for one, that is, the object you pick belongs to you, the object the next person picks belongs to him, etc. Family harmony needs to be really high for this procedure to work.

Today it is often the final total value of the objects each person receives and not the number of objects that governs the emotions and concerns of those chosen to pick. For example, the first person picks an object worth one hundred dollars. The second person picks an object worth three hundred dollars. If the goal is to treat everyone financially equal, the second person owes the first person two hundred dollars if the financial scale is to remain in balance.

FACT Those involved in the selecting process will never agree on what an object is worth.

If you choose to use this method, you may want to assign values to all the objects before the picking takes place, or hire an appraiser to do so. Remind all the pickers that the values you assigned are nonnegotiable. If values have not been preassigned for each object, you may want to have an appraiser present to assign a value to each object as it is picked. The appraiser normally uses wholesale dealer value as his basis, but in this situation it doesn't matter which price basis the appraiser uses, as long as he is consistent. Having the appraiser present at the picking can expose him or her to the anger of family members who don't agree with the values assigned to their choices. Some appraisers may charge more for appraisals in this tense situation.

Once the selection and valuation methods are determined, one final step needs to be taken before the selection begins—deciding who represents whom. Again what seems simple is not.

Assume the executor has decided that the undesignated property in the estate will be divided between the brothers and sisters on an oldest to youngest basis. What happens if one or more of the brothers and/or sisters has died? Does a surviving spouse pick in his or her place? If the spouse also is dead, does a child step in and replace the parent? If there is more than one child, which child makes the pick or is a committee formed? If someone fills in, either spouse or child, do they take their parent's place in line or go to the end of the line because they are the youngest? Any or all these problems and more need to be clarified and resolved before the selection process can begin.

The selection process will proceed smoothly only after you have considered all the questions above. In fact the time you spend dealing with these question can easily exceed the time spent in the selection process. If you did your homework properly, the selection process should be so smooth as to seem almost anticlimactic.

FACT Use multiple selections rather than trying to serve two different constituencies at the same time.

The smaller the number of individuals involved in selection process, the smoother it will be. There is nothing wrong with a person who is downsizing to limit the selection process to his children or those of his children he wishes to include. An executor may choose to limit the selection process only to heirs specified in the deceased's will.

| TIP | No selection process is a solution.

There is nothing in the law that says a selection process has to occur at all. Once the executor has distributed those items designated in the will, he is free to sell everything and distribute the proceeds as cash. Some executors choose to do this as a means of avoiding family squabbles.

The more family and friends you decide to include in the selection process, the more diplomacy is required. Consider the case of grandchildren having access to a grandparent's estate. How are the grandchildren to be treated? The obvious choice appears to be equally. However this approach favors those families with the most children. What happens if a grandchild has died? Does another child in that family get to pick twice? If the answer is no, it is quite possible that that family will feel cheated out of what they consider to rightly be their share of the inheritance.

To Sell or Not to Sell

The assumption thus far has been that the selected goods would transfer for free. However if the person downsizing or the estate needs funds, selling the objects represents an important potential revenue source. Selling is also a method to determine how much a person really wants or values an object.

| FACT | There is absolutely nothing wrong with deciding to sell objects rather than gift them for free.

When selling to family and friends, the standard practice is to price each object, essentially conducting a private tag sale. Usually the value assigned to each object is dealer wholesale or a slight premium above this. The assumption is that the buyers will retain the objects they purchase and not offer them for resale.

Once again a picking order is established. To maintain the appearance of fairness, it is common practice to limit the number of items that can be bought during the initial selection process. Five to ten is a common number for immediate family, two to four for extended family, and one to two for friends. After everyone has selected, subsequent selection rounds are held until no potential buyers remain.

Again, to preserve the appearance of fairness, no price negotiation is allowed. Pleas of "I simply cannot afford it but would love to have it if you will allow me to pay 'x'" must be ignored. Keep the playing field level.

Admittedly the buying process favors those individuals who have money to spend and penalizes those who do not. But if the downsizer or the estate needs money, selling the objects is a reasonable way to proceed.

To Report or Not to Report

When you sell something for financial gain, you legally should report the moneys received as capital gain income.

If you are the executor and sole heir of an estate, you may wish to settle the estate first before selling any personal property to family and friends. If the estate allows, have the personal property valued at replacement value for estate purposes. This provides you with the highest cost basis possible. Assuming you follow this advice, chances are you will wind up selling most of the personal property you inherited at a loss, thus leaving you with no income to claim. Legally, once again, you should report this loss.

There is a little larceny in all our hearts. Cash is a temptation. We assume governing bodies have more than enough money, money which comes out of our pockets, so that a little unreported money is never going to be missed. Chances are this is correct. It also is illegal.

TIP Avoid the temptation to pocket the cash derived from the sale of estate personal property and not report it as income.

An individual downsizing is far more likely to not report the cash derived from selling a collection privately than is an executor handling an estate. In fact, the selection of the selling method used to disperse a collection or estate often hinges on how much of a paper trail the seller wishes to leave behind.

Follow the law. You can bend it a little as long as you stay within its confines. Doing anything beyond that is foolish.

CHAPTER SEVEN

Auction

A UCTION is the most common method used to dispose of a collection or estate. Many see it as the ideal one-step solution. It often is.

There are general auctioneers and auction companies that will sell everything in the house, from antiques to pots and pans to box lots of what you consider junk. When the auction is finished, the home is "broom clean." With real estate value often exceeding the value of the personal property in an estate, a general auction allows the executor to take the house to market in a quick and efficient manner.

FACT There is more than one method to sell real estate. Do not overlook the auction approach.

The auctioning of real estate is a growing trend. The same general auctioneer or auction company that sold your personal property may be the ideal candidate to sell your real estate.

While the auction method of sale may not result in the highest level of return, its quick service and prompt payment more often than not compensates for the lost income. When the amount of time that can be devoted to disposing of a collection or personal property is limited, the auction method of sale is a viable approach.

The Auction Community

We live in an age of specialization. The same applies to the auction community. When most individuals think auction, their mind immediately conjures up the image of an auctioneer selling from the porch or yard of a home or an immaculately dressed individual standing behind the podium of a metropolitan auction house, for example, Christie's or Sotheby's in New York. These are the extremes. There is plenty of variation in between.

Local/Country Auctioneer: A local auctioneer is a generalist who specializes in the sale of all types of household goods. Often self-employed, he may hold a regular or several part-time jobs and do auctioneering on the side. He employs his help on an as-needed basis.

TIP Most local auctioneers are listed in the yellow pages. Do not make the false assumption that those auctioneers who do not have a display advertisement are less specialized or professional.

Often referred to as a "country" or "porch" auctioneer, the local auctioneer may still sell on-site. Check to see if there is a local ordinance or housing development restriction that prohibits this type of auction. Neighbors may not be willing to put up with the traffic and other inconveniences this type of auction causes. Other local ordinances governing parking and signage also should be checked.

Country auctions also are subject to weather variations. The cost to rent a tent to provide backup protection is often difficult to justify. Some auctions take place rain or shine. Others include a rain date in their advertisements. Rain can reduce the crowd by as much as seventy-five percent or more. However there is a select group of buyers who love to go to auctions in the rain. They feel that since the rain keeps the crowd small, the chances to find great buys increases exponentially.

Some local auctioneers are members of the computer and modern communication technology generations, others still insist that the traditional clerk is the way to go. Assuming a computer is properly backed-up, either method should be fine.

Mobile phone bidders are a primary bid group at every auction. If an auction occurs at a place where there is no mobile phone reception, the auctioneer does not have access to a key portion of his buyer base, so it is worth taking that into consideration when deciding whether or not to hold the auction on-site.

Local auctioneers often conduct their auctions in rented fire and social halls. This allows them to provide protection from the weather as well as offer food services to the bidders. A typical local auction lasts for six to eight hours, so food service is essential.

Local auctioneers often will combine several estates into one auction. This increases the quantity and often the quality of the material being offered for sale.

TIP Local auction results tend to be best in late winter and early spring and late summer and early fall.

Local auctioneers are far more likely to schedule an auction for a late afternoon into an evening or on a weekend than are other types of auctioneers or auction houses. This approach allows the general public as well as dealers to attend.

Reusable goods make up the bulk of what the local auctioneer sells. When selling the contents of an estate, antiques and collectibles also are part of the mix. Knowing the drawing power of such items, the local auctioneer lists them in the auction advertisement he places in the local paper.

Local Auction House: A local auction house holds auctions on a weekly or bimonthly basis. The owner and/or staff may be full or part-time. Rarely does it consist of more than two or three full-time staff. The minimum staff at the auction itself is an auctioneer, two clerks, two runners, and a handler. The clerk records the auction's transactions. A handler calls attention to the object being sold, either by holding it up or pointing to it. A runner takes the object to the buyer (new owner) once the hammer falls. Clerks, runners, and handlers usually are hired on a part-time basis. In some cases auctioneers allow volunteers to serve as runners.

The auction is held in a permanent location, often a building devoted to that purpose on a regular basis. A few gallery auctioneers still use a local fire or social hall, preferring to pay rent rather than incur the overhead costs of owning their own building.

Consignment merchandise dominates these auctions. Individuals who are cleaning out an attic, basement, garage, or shed drop off anything they think might have value. Occasionally the gallery will sell an entire estate, and the majority of the auctions involve merchandise from multiple owners.

TIP Look for an auction house that draws a significant crowd of "regulars," the attendees who have reserved seats or arrive early to claim a seat. They are a good indication of a quality auction house.

Auctions at local auction houses generally occur in late afternoons or evenings. Although members of the general public may attend, dealers looking for material they can offer for resale at flea markets, antiques malls, and the Internet usually dominate the crowd. Such auctions are a prime source of material for eBay sellers.

Once again, reusable goods dominate the offerings. The auctioneer sells quickly, eighty to a hundred lots per hour. Because the average price per lot for a sale rarely exceeds fifty dollars, the auctioneer relies on quantity rather than quality to provide his profit.

Regional Auction House: A regional auction house serves a multistate constituency. It has a permanent facility featuring ample parking, several auction gallery rooms, a cataloging area, and storage.

The professional staff of a regional auction house ranges from a dozen to fifty or more employees. In some regional auction houses an auctioneer also assists in the recruitment of material and preparing the material for sale. Other regional houses employ one group of staff members whose sole responsibility is securing merchandise and another whose responsibility is to prepare it for sale. Many of the clerks and floor workers are full-time employees.

Most regional auction houses hold an auction once or twice a month. These houses tend to restrict the material they accept for sale, often having an agreement with a local auctioneer or auction house to auction the material that doesn't interest the larger house.

There are regional auction houses that conduct auctions every week, preferring to offer their clients a full range of services. These weekly auctions involve several auctions, known as rings, that occur simultaneously within the auction house. Separate areas are devoted to art, books, box lots, china and glass, furniture, jewelry, and reusable goods. A weekly specialty, for example, cameras, vintage clothing, coins, firearms, holiday items, postcards, etc., is common. If a private collection is being offered for sale, it becomes the week's specialty.

Regional auction houses also have quarterly catalog sales featuring middle- and high-end antiques, collectibles, and fine arts. When a large private estate or collection is contracted, a specialized catalog sale is scheduled.

TIP Favor an auction house that provides Internet bidding opportunities for a portion or all of its catalog listings.

Regional auction houses also actively participate in bidding by cell phone and the Internet. Many of their sales go to individuals who are not on the bid floor.

Dealers, private collectors, and institutions are the primary buyers at regional auction houses. While these houses continually reach out to the general public, the fact that almost all their sales occur during the business day prevents this constituency from actively participating.

Specialized Auctions: In the twenty-first century, specialty auctions play a major role in the sale of antiques, collectibles, and fine arts. These single collecting category sales are held annually, semi-annually, or as occasion warrants.

The specialists who assemble these sales are often experts in their field of specialization and not auctioneers. When they have assembled enough lots for a sale, usually six hundred or more, they prepare a catalog. A site for the sale is selected and an auctioneer hired for the day or days to call the sales.

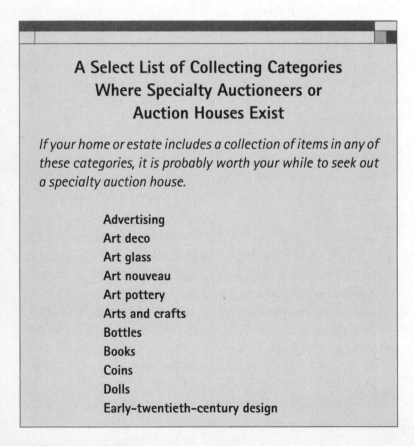

A Select List of Collecting Categories Where Specialty Auctioneers or Auction Houses Exist

If your home or estate includes a collection of items in any of these categories, it is probably worth your while to seek out a specialty auction house.

Advertising

Art deco

Art glass

Art nouveau

Art pottery

Arts and crafts

Bottles

Books

Coins

Dolls

Early-twentieth-century design

Firearms
Hunting and fishing
Majolica
Modernism
Posters
Prints
Railroadiana
Sports cards
Sporting collectibles
Stamps
Stoneware
Toy trains
Toy soldiers
Toys
Western art and cowboy memorabilia
Wallace Nutting

Note 1: Specialized auctions are also conducted at annual collectors' club conventions, so it is worth looking into those auctions as well.

Note 2: This list does not include the specialty catalog sales of regional and national/international auction houses.

Conducting a specialized sale at a large regional auction house is a growing trend. The regional auction house offers a facility, parking, and professional staff designed to specifically serve the auction needs. A few of these auctions still take place in local church, fire, and social halls, but the number lessens each year.

FACT In the age of the Internet, the location of the sale is not as important as worldwide Internet accessibility.

The success of the specialized auction has not been lost on the regional house. More and more regional auction houses are carving out specialized niches, often in direct competition with existing specialists. This is why these specialists are forming partnerships with the regional auction houses.

Specialized auctions usually consist of lots being offered for sale by multiple owners. Many private collectors also turn to these specialists when they feel their collection justifies a single-owner sale.

The majority of lots offered for sale in a specialized auction consist of a single object. Grouping objects into lots occurs when the sale is either a single-owner sale or includes a small- to medium-size collection as part of a catalog offering.

FACT The catalog and prices realized list of a specialized sale is considered a major reference source by collectors.

Most consignment specialized sales contain high-end and some middle-market pieces. The specialist is very selective in the objects he allows in his catalog. When the specialty auction is a single-owner sale, it often includes several hundred lots of commonly found pieces, often grouped in lots of five or more.

Private collectors are the primary buyers at a specialized auction. Competition is often intense. The result is often record-setting prices. One-third to one-half the bidders who participate in a specialized auction place their bids by cell phone or the Internet.

Specialized Auction Houses: The creation of auction houses focusing on one or a very limited number of collecting categories is a major growth area in the antiques, collectibles, and fine arts marketplace. Auction houses specializing in the auction of coins and stamps were the pioneers. In the 1980s the concept spread to sports collectibles. Today specialized auction companies exist in dozens of collecting categories.

The specialized auction company employs a full-time staff of specialists whose principal role is to recruit material. Most of the consignments come from private collectors supplemented by a find or two from others.

These specialized auction companies focus on the upper-middle and high end of the market. They also stress condition and completeness. In addition, they are one of the leading exponents of graded material. Grading services now exist for baseball cards, coins, comic books, and stamps. Many in the auction and collecting community want to expand this concept to other collecting categories, for example, toys. It has not happened yet, but it may in the future.

FACT The pressure to grade is driven by investors, not by collectors.

The expansion of the specialized auction company into the broader antiques, collectibles, and fine arts market is one of the growth trends of the first decade of the twenty-first century. Heritage Coins in Dallas, Texas, is now Heritage Auction Galleries, which bills itself as the largest auctioneer of collectibles in the world. Heritage Gallery is a division specializing in the fine arts. Mastronet, one of the nation's leading sports auctioneers, has become Mastro Auctions. Mastro Auctions also conducts collectibles and fine art auctions.

FACT Investing in antiques, collectibles, and fine arts is not without risk.

While all auctions appeal to both buyers and sellers, those which conduct specialized auctions and the specialized auction company devote a great deal of energy to buyer cultivation. The approach is simple. The objects they sell are really investments, investments that have a track record of appreciating over time. The national/ international auction house also uses this same sales pitch.

National/International Auction House: The 1970s and early 1980s witnessed the arrival of the national/international auction house. Four English houses expanded or franchised their operations to the United States. Everyone knows these names—Bonhams, Christie's, Phillips, and Sotheby's. In America Christie's and Sotheby's are the best known. All are headquartered in New York City. They also have regional offices. Bonhams purchased the remains of Butterfield and Butterfield, located in San Francisco, after eBay was finished playing with it. The Butterfield name still is used, albeit always in conjunction with Bonhams. Everyone expects the Butterfield name to disappear in time, just as did the Parke-Bernet in Sotheby's Parke-Bernet.

The national/international auction houses specialize in the upper middle and high-end antiques, collectibles, and fine art markets. All their auctions are catalog sales.

The staffs are large and departmentalized. A department often includes several specialists. These individuals are so focused on the upper middle and high end of their markets that their market knowledge of commonly found material is very limited.

Overhead costs are enormous. As a result, they set limits on the resale value of lots they accept on consignment. Use two thousand dollars per lot as a working number. The houses will accept lower-valued lots in order to secure high-ticket items.

FACT An object that is just one more object in a crowd at a national/international auction house may be a star in an auction at a strong regional house.

Christie's and Sotheby's have "downstairs" auction galleries for lower-ticket items. However they much prefer, as do the other two auction houses, to encourage consigners to work with regional or local auction sources to dispose of objects for which they have no market.

Buyers consist of international dealers, dealers representing institutions and private collectors, and private collectors. Bidders participate from all over the world. Phone banks for a major sale may consist of twenty phones or more. Multiple staff members are required to keep track of Internet bids.

Selling at Auction

Revisit the piles you created following the guidelines in chapter four. Now that you are aware of the various types of auctions, you should be able to decide very quickly if an auction or auctions is a viable alternative.

However, before searching for an auctioneer or auction house, there are other issues you need to consider.

FACT The more you keep, the more you impact the potential success of the auction.

An auction needs dozens of high-end and upper-middle market objects to attract a large crowd. These are the very objects a person is likely to keep or want to pass down through the family. If you choose the auction sales method, your keep pile should be very small.

TIP Do not be surprised if an auctioneer says no.

Some auctioneers use a minimum gross sales figure to determine if they have any interest in selling a collection or estate. Currently that number is usually ten thousand dollars or more. At a twenty-five percent sales commission, the return to the auctioneer or auction house prior to expenses is twenty-five hundred dollars. Many consider this too low a return for several days of work and the expenses involved.

If a local auctioneer or auction house can combine material from several consignors, he may agree to take the consignment even though it does not meet his ten-thousand-dollar threshold.

If you are planning to use the auction sale method to sell only common household items and lesser-quality goods, it is your responsibility to sort and box them and to take them to a local auctioneer or auction house willing to accept and sell box lots. Not all auction houses do this. It is not fair to ask the auctioneer to do the sorting for you. This type of sorting is time-consuming. Given the amount for which the box lots will sell, the auctioneer or auction house is not even likely to recover its costs.

TIP An auction sales representative can best gauge interest in a sale if what he sees is what he or his organization is going to sell.

No auctioneer or auction house representative likes to visit the site of a potential auction and be told that piece after piece is going to be kept, given to a member of the family, or sold privately. When this occurs, the person cuts his sales visit short and exits with a polite "I am not the right person to be of service to you. Hopefully, you will find someone who is." The chance of the auction sales representative recommending who that person might be is slim to none.

You stand a far better chance of having an auction sales representative agree to conduct a sale if you can say, "What you see is what I am asking you to sell." This means that those objects involved in the sale need to be in a common location. If the objects to be kept or passed down have not been removed, put them in a separate location and keep the door closed.

I have spoken with some auction sales representatives who assure me that they have no problem seeing pieces they are not going to have a chance to auction. They base their decision on what is to be sold. If the auction will be profitable, they will agree to the sale. But as a general rule, it is better to invite the auctioneer to see only the items that are actually available for sale.

Do not expect the auction sales representative to give you an estimate of what he feels the material will bring at auction. There are so many variables involved that the only valid figure is the one at the close of the auction. Any other number is a wild guess.

TIP Beware of auction sales representatives who throw big numbers around.

Some auction sales representatives will provide an estimate of the final sales total as a means of enticing you to sign a contract. If you read the contract, it will specifically state that the value received on the day of the auction is the value of the objects in the auction. Any promised values made prior to the auction are not applicable.

The Cost of Selling at Auction

The auction contract specifies the terms and conditions under which objects are being sold. The auction sales representative will explain the terms and conditions to you. Never sign this contract without reading it thoroughly. In fact, consider having your attorney read it before signing.

FACT Never send your objects to auction without a signed contract.

The question of what the auctioneer is going to charge to sell your objects is a complex one. Most individuals focus on the percentage of the gavel price, that is, the final selling price, the auction will charge.

Historically this ranged from twenty to twenty-five percent. However two developments in the final decades of the twentieth century changed this. First, auction costs rose dramatically, especially in the metropolitan areas. Second, the buyer's penalty (premium) was introduced to give the auctioneer a fixed profit center. The auction community refers to this as a buyer's premium. When I have to pay someone for the right to buy something, I am paying a penalty, not a premium.

A buyer's penalty is the amount an auctioneer or auction house charges a person for the right to buy an object. When first introduced, the buyer's penalty was ten percent of the gavel price. It has slowly crept up to twelve and a half percent, then fifteen percent, and today it stands at twenty percent at many of the major auction houses.

TIP Know an auctioneer's or auction house's buyer's penalty policy before talking with them.

The buyer's penalty works in the seller's favor. By charging the buyer a penalty, the auctioneer or auction house guarantees a fixed percentage of income from the auction. If the auctioneer's or auction house's goal is to average between thirty and thirty-five percent of the gavel price per auction, the higher the buyer's penalty the lower the percentage the auctioneer or auction house has to charge the seller.

In the 1980s and 1990s some of the major auction houses accepted high-end consignments at no cost to the seller. The buyer's penalty on objects above a hundred thousand dollars or more was considered sufficient to cover their costs. If this still occurs, the fact remains carefully hidden. Most major auction houses now charge the seller a minimum of ten percent.

In order for an auctioneer or auction house to survive economically, the accepted percentage of return on the gavel dollars is now thirty-five percent. Thanks to the buyer's penalty, not all that comes from the seller's pocket.

Gone also are the days when the metropolitan auction houses and specialized auctioneers agree to a flat fee based on the final sales total. Local auctions and some small auction houses are the exception. Most still charge a percentage of the sale's total rather than using a sliding cost scale.

When a sliding cost scale is used, each lot is assessed individually. The lower the amount realized when the gavel hits the block, the higher the percentage. The justification is simple. The auctioneer or auction house is aware that it takes just as much effort to sell a twenty-five-dollar object as it does a twenty-five-thousand-dollar object. Time and overhead costs must be recovered.

TIP At least ask if the auctioneer or auction house is willing to base the percentage it charges on the gavel price on the sales total and not the sale of individual items.

If the auctioneer or auction company recognizes that the end value of lots sold will exceed a hundred thousand dollars or more, he may agree to a single flat fee based on the total gavel price. A local auctioneer or auction house will have a lower threshold. It always pays to ask. Do not be surprised if the auctioneer says no.

Other Costs

There are close to a dozen addition costs that auctioneers and auction houses can charge to sellers. Your goal is to keep these charges to a minimum, if not eliminate them entirely.

Each auctioneer or auction house acts differently. As a result, comparing contracts between two competing firms can be like comparing apples to oranges. If you cannot sort through the maze, take the contracts to your lawyer for help.

FACT The percentage of hammer cost is only one of many charges involved in selling at auction.

If the auction is not taking place on your premises or where the estate is located, you can incur two basic costs: (1) packing and (2) transportation to the auction facility. These costs should be clearly specified before you sign an auction contract. Some auctioneers and auction houses charge the seller a higher percentage of the gavel price and include these costs as part of their services. Others keep the percentage low and rely on the hidden charges to boost their bottom line.

FACT The hidden costs are in the fine print.

At on-site auctions, the seller usually pays for the advertising. At auction houses with multiple consigners, it usually is covered by the increase in percentage charge to sell the property. However, read the contract. It should specify the amount of advertising this guarantee covers. If you want additional advertising, for example, in specialized trade periodicals, it is likely to be an additional surcharge.

Who is responsible for insuring the goods to be sold at auction while they are transported, stored, cataloged, and sold? Do not assume you are covered by your household insurance policy. Call your agent and ask. If you ask the auctioneer or auction house to provide the insurance, they will—for a fee. Before agreeing to the fee charged by the auctioneer or auction house, check with your insurance agent to determine if there are temporary personal policy alternatives.

FACT All hidden costs are in addition to the percentage charged on the gavel price.

If a private catalog is being prepared, who is responsible for its production and printing? Do not be surprised if the auctioneer or auction house indicates that the seller is expected to bear this cost. Once again, this is a cost that is often split between the two parties.

If a picture of a seller's object is to appear in a general catalog, there is often a charge assessed. The charge differs if the picture is black and white or color. Charges in excess of a hundred dollars per picture are common. Such charges quickly add up.

Who is responsible for the costs involved in returning unsold objects? In almost every instance the burden is on the seller, especially if the seller has demanded that the object be sold at reserve, that is, setting a minimum price at which the object will be sold. If the object is left to be relisted in a later catalog, there generally is a relisting fee.

Some local auctioneers and auction houses also keep the percentage of the final gavel price paid low by asking the seller to pay for the labor cost for clerks and runners, those who hold up the merchandise during the bidding and deliver it to the successful bidder. Contracts specify the per-hour charge and the number of clerks and runners who will be working. Larger auction houses that sell multiple consignments absorb these costs as part of their overhead. While a fixed time period can often be guaranteed for auction house and gallery auctions, it is difficult to do this when an auction is on-site.

FACT Clearly understand your responsibilities as a seller before signing any contract.

Other costs in conducting an auction can include the price of securing local permits, security personnel, rental cost for the facility, and tents or other special equipment needed to conduct the sale. The list goes on and on. Most of these costs are absorbed by the auctioneer or auction house. However, it always pays to ask.

FACT It is the auctioneer's or his sales representative's responsibility to fully explain the auction procedure, all costs involved, and where this information is found in the contract.

Finding the Right Auctioneer(s) or Auction House(s)

When asked to recommend an auctioneer, I suggest that the person search for (1) an auctioneer who belongs to the National Auctioneers Association and (2) an auctioneer who also is a member of the state auctioneers association. Alas, these two criteria eliminate a good many auctioneers, especially specialized auctioneers.

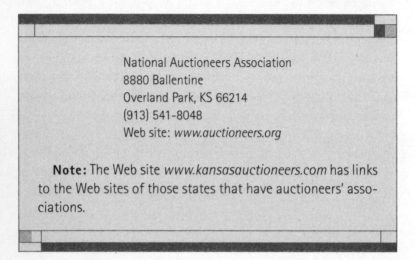

National Auctioneers Association
8880 Ballentine
Overland Park, KS 66214
(913) 541-8048
Web site: *www.auctioneers.org*

Note: The Web site *www.kansasauctioneers.com* has links to the Web sites of those states that have auctioneers' associations.

Not every state licenses auctioneers. If you are selling in a state that does, insist that any auctioneer you engage be licensed. Most states require that the auctioneer include his auction license number in all advertisements and printed material.

States that license auctioneers require them to be bonded. They also require that the auctioneer maintain a separate account into which he must deposit the proceeds from the auction. The consignor or consignors must be paid first before the auctioneer can withdraw any fees or other expenses due.

If you hire an auctioneer in a state that does not require licensing, insist the auctioneer be bonded. Ask to see a copy of his bond before signing a contract. Also insist that he does not commingle auction proceeds with his private accounts. If he does not provide adequate assurances that this is the case, do not hire him.

Before discussing services with an auctioneer or auction house, visit one or more auctions. If the auctioneer or auction house sells by catalog, request copies of two or three catalogs. Do not be surprised if you are asked to pay for them. This is common practice. Make certain the catalogs include a list of the prices realized.

Ask an auctioneer or auction house to send you a copy of his sale brochure and/or credentials in advance. Many auctioneers and auction houses have Web sites. Review them thoroughly.

Ask around. Auctioneers and auction houses rely heavily on word of mouth to generate new clients. Every auctioneer or auction house has a bad day. If the first review is negative, ask again. Be concerned only if a negative pattern develops.

TIP Resist all pressure to sign a contract until you are ready.

As you do your research, one auctioneer or auction house may stand out from all the rest in respect to the type of personal property or collection you wish to sell. While it pays to comparison shop, you do not have to do this when the choice is clear.

Assuming you select the auction sales method, you may want to consider using several different auctioneers or auction houses. The goal is to sell your collection or personal property in the market where its value will be maximized. If you have items that should be sold by one of the major New York City auction houses, send them to New York.

If using multiple auctioneers or auction houses, first contact the specialized and national/international auctioneers or auction houses. These firms will cherry-pick what you have to sell. While normally one would resist cherry-picking, it is acceptable at this point.

Remember the piles you created based on the advice in chapter four? The antiques, collectibles, and fine arts piles were designed to allow a multiple auction house approach.

FACT A professional auctioneer is a skilled adviser.

Select an auctioneer or auction house based upon its professional competence and level of performance. Equally important is finding an auctioneer or specialists within an auction house with whom you can work comfortably.

Once you have selected the auctioneer or auction house, trust his advice. The auctioneer's or auction house's goal is identical to your goal—maximize the financial return of the objects being sold. You have done your job, let them do theirs. The more you interfere, the harder it will be for the auctioneer or auction house to function.

Should You Attend?

Do not attend the auction or auctions where your collection or property is being sold. Stay home, take a trip, or otherwise keep yourself occupied.

If you attend the auction, you will regret it. All you will remember are those lots that sold for less than you thought they were worth. You will forget entirely about those lots that brought two and three times what you thought they would.

Once you have made the decision to sell, what difference does it make what each object realized? The final amount payable to you at the end of the auction should be the focus of your concerns.

TIP If you do decide to attend the auction, do not bid. Some auctioneers and auction houses specifically forbid this.

If you attend the auction, your hand will fly in the air, mimicking a knee-jerk action, the minute the first piece you see is selling for less than you think it is worth. "I will keep it before I see it sell for that" is governing your actions. Bad, bad, bad! Further, if a seller starts bidding and does not win the item, other buyers are immediately going to accuse the seller, auctioneer, or auction house of sanctioning shilling. Again, bad, bad, bad!

Simply put, you are a distraction if you attend the auction. The auctioneer or auction house feels they need to assign someone to watch over you. Buyers who know you will want to visit and chat instead of paying attention to the auction proceedings. They may even offer to do a better deal with you privately if you withdraw an object from the auction.

TIP Stay home. Everyone benefits.

One More Possibility

What happens if you have a houseful of items but their value is too low to attract the services of an auctioneer or auction house. When this occurs, the possibility of holding an estate sale is eliminated. A garage sale is a possibility, but you do not want to go to the trouble.

Some local auctioneers offer a service whereby they buy the contents of a house and leave it "broom clean." The amount they pay is small. In fact, be thrilled if they are willing to pay something rather than charging a fee to complete the task.

Cleaning and sorting material is hard work. It is a dirty, time-consuming business. Those individuals who buy estates and leave a house "broom clean" earn their money the old-fashioned way—through hard work.

Bank trust officers and estate attorneys who act as executors are fond of working with such individuals. Bank trust officers and estate attorneys also tend to favor a specific local auctioneer or auction house if the contents of an estate justify employing one. The goal, especially for bank trust officers, is to clear the real estate as quickly as possible. When time is weighed against maximizing the economic potential, time usually is the winner.

Auction is one sale method for selling a collection and disposing of personal property. There are others which will be explained in upcoming chapters. Some involve hiring a skilled professional. Others are do-it-yourself projects. You need to keep searching until you find the answer that is right for you.

CHAPTER EIGHT

Estate Sale

IS this an estate sale or tag sale? The answer depends on where in the United States you are located. In portions of New England and other scattered locations across the United States, tag sale is synonymous with garage sale. The garage sale method is discussed in the next chapter.

When used properly, estate sale refers to a sale involving prepriced items belonging to a single owner. Occasionally an estate sale may include objects from other consignors, but the number of consignors usually does not exceed two or three.

FACT The term "house sale," when used to refer to the sale of personal property, is synonymous with estate sale.

Technically an estate sale should involve property from an individual who is deceased, but the term is used broadly. The property may also be the result of downsizing.

An estate sale generally takes place in a home. Once again, there are exceptions. If the estate sale professional feels the home is too small to adequately showcase the property, the property may be moved to a nearby rental facility.

Implied in estate sale is the understanding that the property consists mainly of antiques, collectibles, fine arts, and brand-name reusables. Dealers attend estate sales looking for merchandise to add to their inventory. Newcomers to the community attend estate sales to find quality merchandise cheaper than new. Estate sale regulars are looking for hidden treasures.

💎 FACT Estate sale professional equals estate liquidation manager.

Estate sales are conducted by estate sale professionals, also known as estate liquidation managers, most of whom work part-time. As the demand increases for professional assistance in disposing of a deceased's estate when the executor lives hundreds or thousands of miles away, a small group of full-time estate sale professionals has emerged. At the moment most of these individuals and small firms are located in the East Coast megalopolis and other large metropolitan areas.

The use of an outside professional is one element that differentiates estate sales from garage sales. The seller is usually responsible for conducting a garage sale. Can private individuals conduct an estate sale? Of course, they can, if they have the field knowledge of how to price the merchandise. If they do not, the end result will be disastrous.

Is an Estate Sale the Right Choice?

A strong estate sale environment and a strong auction sale environment rarely exist in the same region. In an area where estate sales are strong, auctions tend to be weak. In areas where estate sales are weak, auctions tend to be strong. Estate sale professionals compete with auctioneers for the same business. Little wonder a high level of animosity exists between them.

Chances are you know the sales method that is prevalent in your area. If you are the executor of an estate and unfamiliar with the area in which the sale will occur, consult with your attorney, family who live nearby, and/or friends and neighbors.

💎 FACT Local papers tend to run auction and estate sale advertisements on a set day each week. Thursday and Friday are the two most popular days. However check a full week's worth of newspaper classifieds to make certain.

A quick check of the local paper also will provide the answer. If the paper is loaded with auction advertising, think auction. If estate sale advertising dominates the paper, think estate sale. Again check the local meaning for estate sale. If the advertisement reads "estate/tag sale," chances are it is an advertisement for a garage sale.

Estate sale implies the sale contains a higher grade of merchandise than that found in a garage sale. This is another way the two sales methods differ. However the primary purpose of an estate sale is to leave the house "broom clean," just as if an auction was conducted. As a result the estate sale manager is responsible for disposing of everything from high-end to low-end, from salable to disposable.

Most estate sales occur on-site. If you are downsizing, you need to decide if you are willing to put up with a week or more of inconvenience during the organization process, sale, and cleanup. If the estate sale is disposing of the personal property of an estate, this is not a concern.

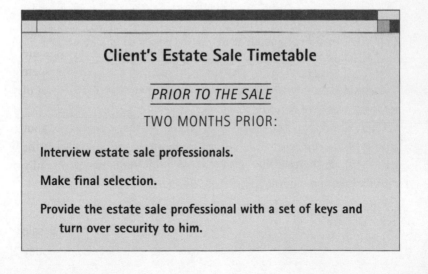

Client's Estate Sale Timetable

PRIOR TO THE SALE
TWO MONTHS PRIOR:

Interview estate sale professionals.

Make final selection.

Provide the estate sale professional with a set of keys and turn over security to him.

SIX WEEKS PRIOR:

Identify any pieces that will be offered for sale first to family and friends and set times for their visits.

Box and prepare for storage all personal and family items that will not be offered for sale.

FOUR WEEKS PRIOR:

Review all advertising, brochures, and flyers with the estate sale professional.

Provide a list of all individuals you wish to receive information about the sale.

Start touting the sale among friends, at service clubs, in fact, whenever you are out in public.

TWO WEEKS PRIOR:

Review the sales plan with the estate sales professional.

Answer any final questions he may have about the objects being sold.

Inform the neighbors that the sale will take place.

TWO DAYS PRIOR:

Take one last walk through the house and say good-bye to the items.

Do a final review with the estate sale professional.

SALE

Disappear. Take a trip.

Do not check with the estate sale professional hourly, morning, noon, and night, or at the end of each day.

AFTER THE SALE

FIRST WEEK:

Expect a preliminary accounting within twenty-four to forty-eight hours.

Review the plans to dispose of unsold items with the estate sale professional.

FOURTH WEEK:

Expect a final accounting.

Write a letter of recommendation for the estate sale professional if you are pleased with the job he did.

Finding an Estate Sale Professional

Most estate sale professionals rely on referrals, either from an attorney, bank trust officer, or satisfied customer, or from newspaper advertisements. Yellow page listings usually include these individuals in the auction listings. Few editions have separate listings for estate sales.

TIP The local chamber of commerce, moving companies, and real estate companies are other sources of referrals.

Prior to talking to an estate sale professional, try to attend one or more of the estate sales conducted by this individual. Resist the temptation to just look at the prices. Check the layout, traffic flow, number of customers, security, and checkout procedure. Talk to buyers as they leave and ask them to critique their shopping experience.

Estate sale professionals should be able to provide a sales kit, résumé, or both. Ask for a list of customer references. Since most estate sales result in a "broom-clean" environment, client confidentiality and privacy concerns that apply to appraisers in respect to disclosing information about clients do not apply. Assume the estate sale professional would not include a person on the list without asking his permission first.

Conduct personal interviews on-site. Include a tour of the home and carefully go over with the estate sale professional exactly what you want sold. Obtain a copy of the contract and have the estate sale professional explain its terms and conditions. Inquire if there are other services you might receive that are not specified in the contract.

TIP Beware of those estate sale professionals who tell you they are "out of the box" thinkers.

After the tour and as the interview ends, ask the estate sale professional for a rough idea as to how they would handle the sale of your property if selected. There is a traditional, standard approach to conducting an estate sale—a one- or two-day event with all merchandise marked and buyers admitted on a controlled basis. Continued success has proven the validity of this approach, but a little creative thinking may add to the possibility of success. However avoid agreeing to any "new" approach. In this instance stick to the tried and true.

TIP When signing a contract for any sales service, make certain it has an escape clause just in case you and the person with whom you contracted reach a point of major disagreement on policy and/or procedures.

Finally, the estate sale professional is going to be intimately involved in your life for two to four weeks. Select a person who has a personality and style with which you are comfortable. If you cannot work with a person who is authoritative and demanding, then do not hire someone who is.

The Cost

Most estate sale professionals charge a percentage of the final total sales. In the 1990s this charge ranged from twenty-five to thirty percent. Today the charge is more likely to be thirty to thirty-five percent. Some sale professionals charge as high as forty percent.

FACT A higher percentage fee that is all-inclusive may be a better deal than a lower percentage fee with additional charges.

Typically the fee is all-inclusive. There are no extra charges. However the percentage only covers the basics. If you as a seller want extras over and above the basic package, you should expect to pay for them.

Do not be surprised if you interview several estate sale professionals and find that their fee structure is basically the same. The community of individuals who sell antiques, collectibles, and fine arts is relatively small. Everybody knows everybody else's business. If you do discover a variation in fees, it is likely to be very small.

The Services You Should Expect

You have hired your estate sale professional. It is time to put them to work. It also is time for you to step aside and let them work. You have hired the estate sale professional because he knows his business. Let him do it.

◆ | FACT | Use the contract as a guide to make certain you receive the services promised.

The contract sets the date of sale, usually one to two months in advance. Estate sales tend to occur more quickly than an auction, although there are plenty of cases where the opposite is true.

If the estate sale involves the sale of the estate of the deceased, the estate sale professional generally assumes the responsibility for the security of the real estate and contents upon the signing of the contract. If the sale is the result of downsizing and the client still is living in the house, the estate sale professional may have no security obligations until the sale preview or, if no preview, the start of the sale.

A month prior to the sale, the estate sale individual should prepare the advertising. Most will review it with the client. This is done more as a courtesy than obligation. Advertising for estate sales, and most local auctions as well, occurs a week to ten days in advance of the sale.

An estate sale professional is expected to provide all the equipment required to conduct the sale, from that which is needed to clean objects and location to office and other checkout equipment needed to conduct the sale. The cost for this equipment is borne by the estate sale professional.

◆ | TIP | Before hiring an estate sale professional for appraisal purposes, make certain he is qualified.

Some estate sale professionals supplement their income by offering appraisal services. If you still need appraisals for pieces that are being kept or gifted to individuals from an estate, make arrangements with the estate sale professional to do this. Appraisal services are not included in the standard package of services from an estate sale professional. Expect to pay extra.

It is the responsibility of the estate sale professional to provide all the help needed to conduct the sale. Resist any temptation to volunteer your assistance as a method of reducing the cost. You do not know what you are doing. The staff of the estate sale professional does. You will be of far greater service if you disappear two days prior to the sale and return one day afterward.

The estate sale professional is responsible for preparing the items for sale. The first task will be to sort the objects and advantageously place them throughout the house and garage. The location may not make sense to you, but it does to the professional.

Preparation involves more than sorting. Objects sold at estate sales need to be "room ready," that is, taken by the buyer from the estate sale and placed in a location in their new home ready for use. Cleaning objects can range from simple dusting to taking vintage clothing and other textiles to the dry cleaner to polishing the silver. If done correctly, your home and its objects will have never looked as good as on the eve of the sale.

TIP The goal is to sell as much as possible, ideally everything.

The estate sale professional is responsible for pricing and tagging all the objects. Do not second guess the prices. Every time you insist on a price being increased, you reduce the chance of the object being sold.

Estate sale prices tend to be halfway between retail and wholesale. Some estate sale professionals price objects at twenty percent of book/retail value, with the intention of gradually reducing the price if the object does not sell. Today this practice is risky.

An estate sale works best (1) when the crowd is so large that a buying frenzy prevails and (2) when the sale appears loaded with bargains. There is no guarantee the first will occur. Setting lower prices can make the second happen, resulting in a greater total profit.

The estate sale professional conducts the sale. The person you hired, not a member of his staff, should be present throughout the sale. The estate sale professional is your representative.

The Family and Specialist Buyers

You will be pressured by family and friends asking for the right to visit the sale prior to the general public and buy objects of interest. Assume that no matter how hard you try, you will not be able to say no to everyone.

FACT Buyers will stay away from an estate sale that they think has been picked over by family or preferred customers.

The estate sale professional and client must agree to the list of individuals who will have the right to buy items prior to the sale. If this is going to happen, it needs to be done early in the process. The individuals make their selection. The estate sale professional sets the price. The value of these early purchases is added to final sales total. The estate sale professional deserves a commission for providing his expertise.

This presale needs to take place before the estate sale professional prepares the sale's advertising copy, brochures, and flyers. Buyers have been known to riot when objects listed in an advertising piece are not available when the public sale begins.

TIP Some object categories sell better to specialized dealers than to the general public.

There are a select number of collecting categories where an estate sale professional may bring in a specialty buyer rather than offer the items for public sale. Books, coins, firearms, records, and stamps are a few examples. When a specialty buyer is brought in early, the buyer is expected to buy all the examples available for one lot price.

Do not allow an estate sale specialist to bring in a jewelry dealer in advance. Jewelry is a big seller and draws a crowd. Antique and costume jewelry sells equally well at an estate sale. Further, the more jewelry, the bigger the buying audience is likely to be. Many of these jewelry hunters will also buy other items.

How an Estate Sale Works

The advertising has been placed, everything is priced, and the sale is about to begin. A final check is made to make certain everything is priced, the traffic patterns established, security is in place, and the checkout counters manned.

Customers line up outside and receive a number. This determines the order in which they enter the sale site. The standard policy is between forty and fifty customers initially with a new customer being allowed to enter when one of the customers leaves.

FACT Crowd control begins at the door.

Pressure from those waiting to enter is intense. The person assigned to maintain order at the entrance is critical. Rules must be applied universally. Controlling the number of buyers inside reduces security concerns and delays at checkout. It is the traditional approach, and the one I favor.

Ownership of an object occurs at the moment of purchase. This rule is bent slightly at estate sales. Ownership is understood the moment an individual signs his or her name on the sales tag. Equally

The Feeding of the Piranha—
A Case Study

Gary Miller and Scotty Mitchell, owners of Millchell, Inc., located in Fort Worth, Texas, are the consummate estate sale professionals. I know none better. Whenever I offer a course on how to conduct estate sales through my Institute for the Study of Antiques and Collectibles, I check to see if Gary and Scotty are available to teach. Check them out via their Web site, *www.millchell.com.*

Most estate sale professionals use a controlled admittance policy when conducting a sale. Gary and Scotty occasionally take just the opposite approach. When the sale is ready to begin, they open the door and let everyone in. They call this "the feeding of the piranha." Letting all the buyers in at once creates a frenzy of buyers snatching up pieces eager to find bargains, and that energy yields great sales results.

Although this isn't the method I recommend, it does yield excellent results for Gary and Scotty—and I could listen forever to the stories they tell about this practice. My biggest concern is that I will die laughing.

understood is that the customer is expected to pay for any item so designated. There are those individuals at any estate sale who grab anything in which they think they may have an interest and put it on a pile with the intention of sorting through it later. Estate sale employees must do everything in their power to prevent this. "Are you absolutely certain you are buying that?" is a question that needs to be asked repeatedly.

Most estate sales occur over a two- or three-day weekend. This encourages the general public to attend. Dealers would prefer the sale was held during the week, thus eliminating competition from those whose work prevents them from attending. Obviously you want your estate sale to occur on a weekend.

FACT Estate sales rely on the sales principle that you need to buy it now because it may not be here when you return tomorrow.

Prices tend to remain firm the first day. Offers are taken with the understanding that they will be considered only at the conclusion of the sale. Beginning on the second day if the estate sale is two days in length, a gradual reduction of prices occurs. The first reduction is ten percent. The reduction can reach as high as fifty percent in the final hour of the sale. If the estate sale is three days in length, the reduction generally begins in the middle of the second day and occurs over a much longer period.

Those estate sale employees working the floor are salespeople as well as security personnel. They should be skilled in closing a sale. Their demeanor should suggest that of a professional adviser, a person whose word can be trusted.

Title to an object passes when a buyer pays the seller. When a buyer is finished "shopping" the estate sale, he gathers those objects that he has put his name on and the objects on the pile he has set aside and takes them to the checkout area. He pays for his purchases as a single unit.

TIP Your estate sale professional should make it clear before admitting buyers that putting their name on an object or placing an object in a pile is a commitment to buy.

Seasoned estate sale buyers often abuse the "name on the object" and "pile" privilege. Before paying they review the objects they have set aside and divide them into two groups—those they really want and those they were only considering. They remove their names from the latter and put them back in the sale. Obviously this is not in the best interest of the seller and should not be permitted.

Buyers take the objects they want to purchase to the cashier. The tag price at the time prevails. There is no price negotiation. If a buyer asks for a volume discount, the answer is no. Once again, make certain this will be clearly understood by buyers before they enter the sale.

Accepting left bids is a common practice at estate sales. If the item remains unsold at the conclusion of the sale, the estate sale professional consults with the owner. If the owner accepts the left bid, the estate sale professional contacts the buyer and makes the necessary arrangements to have the buyer pick up and pay for the object. In most cases the client allows the estate sale professional to make the judgment call.

Goods are sold at an estate sale based on an "all sales are final" basis. Further, as at auction, goods are sold "as is." It is the responsibility of the buyer to check the object before buying it. However it is equally the responsibility of those preparing material for sale to mark or somehow point out any defects discovered in an object.

FACT "No" is the proper response to someone who wants to return something.

No returns are allowed at an estate sale. No matter how clearly this policy is stated, there always are individuals who think it does not apply to them. They are wrong, and they need to be told so.

FACT Any money is better than no money.

A fair amount of wheeling and dealing takes place in the final hour of the sale. Those buyers who remain will often make offers to buy at ten to twenty percent of the tag price. If the object is a common one, it makes far more sense to say yes than no. The goal from the beginning was to sell everything.

The Aftermath

I have yet to learn of an estate sale where every piece sold during the period of the sale. There always is material left. The contract you signed with the estate sale professional should contain a clear set of guidelines for disposing of what is left.

Most estate sale professionals know individuals who buy the remains of an estate sale. They do not offer much, but the objects are gone.

Some objects can be donated to charity. The estate sale professional should box them, deliver them, and present you with the receipt.

TIP Come to a clear understanding before the sale about who is responsible for absorbing bad checks.

You should expect a preliminary report of the sale's proceeds within twenty-four to forty-eight hours after the sale and a full accounting and payment within thirty days. There are many reasons for the delay. Checks need to clear. Individuals who have left offers need to be contacted and arrangements made for them to pick up and pay for their objects. Everyone needs time to clear their heads and, hopefully, celebrate a successful sale.

Salting a Sale

When the public attends an estate sale, the assumption is that all the items being offered for sale are from a single estate. If this is not the case, the estate sale professional needs to clearly state this in all the literature.

There is a second public assumption that opens the door to problems. The public also assumes that all the objects in the house are old, that is, they have been there for a period of years. They do not even want to consider the possibility that this is not the case.

TIP Do not judge everyone involved in the selling of antiques, fine arts, and collectibles by the few rotten apples in the barrel.

Unfortunately there are some unscrupulous estate sale professionals and auctioneers who buy modern reproductions (exact copies of period pieces), copycats (stylistic copies of period pieces), fantasy items (items that appear to be historic but are brand-new), and fakes (objects deliberately meant to deceive). These unscrupulous sellers remove the stickers and any other indications that the objects are new. If the object appears too new they may age or damage them slightly to make the object appear older than it is. The objects are then placed throughout the house.

FACT Jewelry is perhaps the most salted of the collecting categories.

These unscrupulous sellers hide behind two principles. First, their terms of sale indicate all objects are sold on an "as is" basis. Second, *caveat emptor*, let the buyer beware, is the law that applies. The burden is on the buyer to know what he is buying, not the seller to explain what he is selling.

If asked about the authenticity of an object, the unscrupulous seller parries with vague phrases such as: "I am no expert, you decide"; "It looks okay to me, but it is your call"; and "It was here when I started pricing the material." In respect to the last statement, the unscrupulous dealer is merely bending the truth. He brought the reproductions, copycats, fantasy items, and fakes into the house before he began the pricing process.

FACT Avoid any seller who suggests he can increase the income from your sale by sharing the profits made from the sale of reproductions, copycats, fantasy items, and fakes.

Thanks to an increased sophistication among today's buyers, the number of unscrupulous auctioneers and estate sale professionals has diminished considerably. Use your best judgment in determining if the person you hired is honest and reliable. If you suspect they are not, talk to your attorney. If you can confirm your suspicions, then fire this person and hire someone else.

Moving Forward

An auction or estate sale works best when the personal property offered for sale contains a large number of quality items. While an estate sale professional will consider an estate sale that will result in four thousand to five thousand dollars of gross sales, an auctioneer needs to double or triple these numbers. A regional auction house considers a sale that grosses less than fifty thousand dollars as unsuccessful. Their preferred number is a hundred thousand dollars plus.

What happens if you have a house full of objects or a collection that is simply not going to meet any of these thresholds? Are you dead in the water? Absolutely not! There are several other alternatives, which we will discuss in the next chapters.

CHAPTER NINE

Garage Sale

YOU have a large quantity of things that are too good to throw out but not strong enough to attract an auctioneer or estate sale professional. It is time to consider a garage sale.

What is a garage sale? A garage sale is a venue to turn your recyclables and reusables into cash. Just because the objects you are selling have no immediate or future use to you does not mean others feel the same way. In fact, what you are selling may be the very thing they need.

Let's clear the air in respect to garage sale nomenclature. A rummage sale, tag sale, white elephant sale, yard sale, or whatever term is commonly used in your location is a garage sale. Further, a garage sale does not have to occur in a garage. It can be held in a driveway, yard, park, community center, you name it. It is the type of merchandise and sale price point that determines whether or not the event in question is a garage sale.

Set Goals

Getting rid of everything you planned to sell is your primary goal. Ideally this means everything sells. Realistically the chances of this happening are slim. Your final act of the day may be placing the remaining unsold items in cartons at the edge of the driveway or curb with a note reading "FREE."

FACT You need only one goal—be rid of everything by day's end.

Consider setting a monetary goal. Make it a conservative one. The adage "don't spend your money before you have it" applies. A conservative monetary goal works to your advantage. Once you meet that goal, you can immediately reduce prices dramatically to increase the possibility that the objects will sell.

FACT All money received from the sale of garage-sale merchandise is money you did not have when the sale started.

Garage sales are hard work. Your challenge is to make your garage sale fun. Most individuals take garage sales far too seriously. They forget that they already have decided that the material they are offering for sale has no value to them. They could have saved their time and trouble by taking the material to the landfill. Instead they opted to sell it. Plan from the beginning to celebrate and not collapse in exhaustion while thanking God it is over when your garage sale ends.

Getting Ready for the Sale

There are no garage sale professionals. Garage sales are run by amateurs, many of whom have only a minimal knowledge of how a garage sale should be conducted. Do not reinvent the wheel. Your local bookstore has several garage sale manuals you can buy. Some newspapers provide a free garage sale kit when you place a classified advertisement in the paper for your garage sale. The quickest method to learn how to conduct a garage sale is to visit garage sales in the area in which you will be selling and observe what they are doing and whether or not it is working.

Checklist of What to Look for
When Checking Out Garage Sales

1. Types and placement of signs

2. Sale layout

3. Types of merchandise that are selling

4. Grouping of objects

5. Display techniques

6. Parking issues

7. Crowd control

8. Seller and customer interaction

9. Security

10. Location of cashier and method of payment

11. What does not appear to be working

12. Talk with customers, but only after they are done shopping, and ask them what type of items are they seeking.

There is no right or wrong way to run a garage sale. The choices of how to conduct a garage sale number in the hundreds. The right choice is the one that works for you.

TIP Buyers judge the quality of the items offered at a garage sale by the piece in the worst condition. Keep the quality of what you are selling as high as possible.

You already have selected the objects that will be in your garage sale. You did this when you organized your piles. You do not have to hunt through the house looking for material you would like to sell. Nonetheless take a few minutes and do a final walk-through. Pay close attention to the "junk" pile. You might want to select a few items and try selling them at your garage sale before junking them.

What Should Not Be Sold at a Garage Sale

Antiques, collectibles, and fine arts, on the one hand, and junk, on the other, are the two categories of objects that should not be sold at a garage sale.

Garage sale buyers expect to pay five to ten cents on the dollar for the objects they buy. While antiques, collectibles, and fine arts are sold at wholesale, the wholesale price for these items is much higher. An antique should realize between thirty and forty percent of retail, a collectible between twenty and thirty percent, and a quality piece of fine art between fifty and sixty percent. You will not achieve these prices at a garage sale. There are other sale venues at which you will do much better.

There is an exception. If you have a limited number of antiques, collectibles, and fine arts items and have done your price research properly, you may wish to give them a try at your garage sale. They will be a good draw even if they do not sell.

Chapter one contains definitions for what constitutes an antique and collectible. Here is another method. If you are sixty-five years old, follow these rules: (1) if the object belonged to the generations that came before you, it is an antique, (2) if the object is from your childhood or young adulthood, it is an antique, (3) if your children are over forty-five and they played with the object as youngsters, it is an antique, and (4) if the object is from your grandchildren and they are over thirty, it is a collectible. Finally, check to see if the object fits one of the standard collecting categories in a general antiques and collectibles price guide. If it does, hold it back and use another method to dispose of it.

TIP The standard ten-year rule may not apply in this instance.

When conducting a garage sale for purposes other than downsizing or settling an estate, the typical rule is to sell primarily objects that are ten years old or less. When downsizing and selling for estate purposes, you need to adopt an "everything on the pile goes" rule. Some of the reusables, such as utilitarian objects, will be over ten years old.

In deciding whether or not an object belongs in the garage sale or junk pile, ask yourself two basic questions: (1) Is it something I would use? and (2) Can I think of anyone who might use it? If you answer no to both, review it a second time. Obviously you are selling it because you have no use for it. You also cannot know everything. If the object is in very good or better condition and complete, leave it in the garage sale.

TIP The garage sale objects that sell best are those that are ready to be taken to their new home and used.

If an object is broken beyond repair, incomplete, rusted, and/or shows signs of very heavy use, send it to the landfill. The age of fixer-uppers is over. Once again, there are a few exceptions—lawn mowers and snowblowers are one such category. There are retired individuals who love buying these items and fixing them for resale. The popularity of DIY programs and books also indicates that people are interested in bargains in furniture for refinishing, so furniture may sell even if badly in need of paint.

Pricing the Objects for Sale

The rule is simple. Price the object to sell. If it does not sell, you set the price too high. This is why you will need to adjust your prices several times during the course of the sale.

 Do not get greedy. The goal is to sell, not to keep.

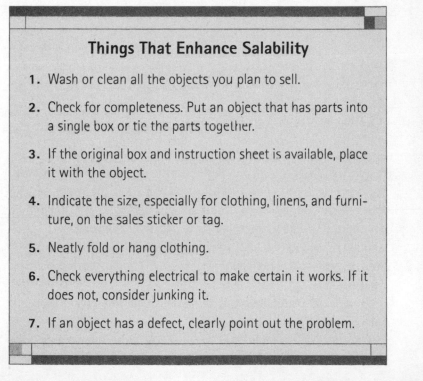

Things That Enhance Salability

1. Wash or clean all the objects you plan to sell.

2. Check for completeness. Put an object that has parts into a single box or tie the parts together.

3. If the original box and instruction sheet is available, place it with the object.

4. Indicate the size, especially for clothing, linens, and furniture, on the sales sticker or tag.

5. Neatly fold or hang clothing.

6. Check everything electrical to make certain it works. If it does not, consider junking it.

7. If an object has a defect, clearly point out the problem.

There are no fixed values for garage sale objects, just as there are no fixed values of antiques, collectibles, and fine arts. An object that just sold for a dollar at one garage sale might bring five dollars at another. Price is very much a factor of time, place, and moment.

Forget nickels and dimes whenever possible, and think in terms of quarters, half dollars, and dollars. Nickels and dimes complicate the selling process, if for no other reason than they create a hassle when making change.

You are running a garage sale, not a store in a shopping mall. Prices such as $16.49 or $29.99 make no sense. Keep it simple. Use prices that allow you to make change in quarters and dollar bills.

The following pricing structure is recommended:

SALE PRICE	INCREMENT
$0.00 to $2.00	twenty-five cents
$2.00 to $10.00	fifty cents
$10.00 to $20.00	dollar
$ 20.00 to $100.00	five dollars
Above $100.00	twenty-five dollars

FACT Overpricing is the biggest mistake that sellers make.

It is hard to be objective and put personal feelings aside. In addition, there is a little greed in all of us. We want the most, not the least, we can get. When you think the price is too low, it probably is just right. Remember, your goal is to get rid of the stuff.

There are no garage sale price guides. You have to rely on your own instinct and what you found similar goods sold for at other garage sales.

There usually are numerous garage sales on any given weekend. The competition is fierce. You want your prices to be the lowest. If true, the rumor that there are bargains galore at your garage sale will spread like wildfire among the garage sale regulars and buyers on the hunt that day.

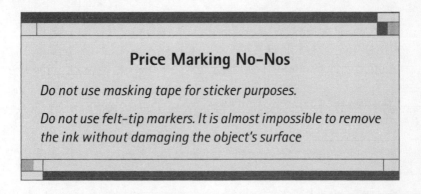 **FACT** As a seller, you are responsible for placing a price on all objects.

The price you put on an object is your offer to sell. Buyers walk away from garage sales where items are not priced. No one likes being sized up by a seller whose purpose is trying to guess the highest price the buyer will pay.

When marking an object, you have two goals: (1) make the price easy to read and locate and (2) place the price on the object in a method that will not damage the object. Do not put a sticker or marker on an object that cannot be easily removed. Glued stickers often leave residue. Select and use them carefully.

Price Marking No-Nos

Do not use masking tape for sticker purposes.

Do not use felt-tip markers. It is almost impossible to remove the ink without damaging the object's surface

---

Pin tags on clothing and linens. To save time, divide all textiles into three to six price categories and use a different colored dot to represent each category. Create a large chart showing the colored dot and the value it represents.

Use sticker labels on ceramic, glass, metal, and wood objects. Buy stickers that state they can be removed without damaging an object. Do not apply stickers on surface decoration. Decoration is often done over the glaze, for example, all gold on ceramics and glass. A buyer will not be thrilled if some of the surface decoration is lost when the sticker is removed. In fact, the buyer will no longer be a buyer.

Mark paper products, for example, jigsaw puzzles, magazines, photographs, etc., with a soft pencil. Marking them on the back or bottom is preferable. Never use labels of any kind.

Consider creating quarter, fifty-cent, and one-dollar boxes and tables. Again, use a color code to identify which price applies to which object. This will greatly simplify the job of your cashier.

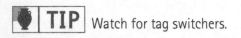 **TIP** Watch for tag switchers.

Tag switchers are individuals who exchange the tag on a higher-priced object with a tag taken off a lower-priced piece. Tag switchers are a fact of life at garage sales. If someone brings an object to you or your cashier and the price marked on it does not seem to make sense, tell the buyer you mispriced it, apologize, and withdraw it from the sale. Your defense is simple. Everyone makes mistakes. Apologize, but stand your ground.

TIP If you are not acting as the cashier at your garage sale, walk the person or persons who will through your sale about an hour prior to opening to familiarize them with your pricing.

Setting the Time and Date

Check the local rules and regulations. Call the municipal authority to see what rules apply to holding a garage sale. At the very least, there will be rules about posting and removing signage. A temporary permit to hold the sale, restriction on Sunday sales, and parking restrictions are other regulations that may apply.

TIP Do not schedule a garage sale on the same weekend as a major local or national sporting event, local festival, or graduation. On the other hand, it may be wise to schedule a garage sale to coincide with a local or regional antique event or antiques car show. These events produce the buyers you want.

Every area has its ideal garage sale season. In the North, Midwest, and West, the ideal time is mid-April until late May and then again from mid-August until late September. While it is possible to hold garage sales on a year-round basis in the South and Southwest, there are periods that are better than others, such as when the retiree community is in town.

FACT One day is more than enough time to get the job done.

Most garage sales last two days—Saturday and Sunday. The critical question is do you need two days? The answer is no. Most of the second day is spent sitting idly waiting for customers. Saturday is the ideal day for a garage sale. What happens if it rains? Reschedule your garage sale for the next Saturday. Avoid using Sunday as a rain date. A Sunday sale makes it tough for the church crowd to attend in the morning.

Before setting the date, check with the neighbors to make certain there is no conflict. You do not want to hold your garage sale at the same time your neighbor's daughter is getting married in their backyard.

If you are lucky the area where you live or in which the estate is located is home to an annual or semiannual neighborhood or multi-family garage sale. Schedule your garage sale at the same time. Neighborhood and multifamily garage sales draw large crowds.

Once you tell the neighbors about your garage sale, some may want to tag along, that is, hold their own sale on the same day or weekend. Encourage them to do this. Offer to split the cost of advertising.

▼ TIP Say no to anyone who asks you to add a few of their pieces to your garage sale.

Consigned material is nothing but a headache. How do you keep track of it? Who is responsible if a piece is stolen? The consignor expects you to sell his things without charging him a fee. After all, what are friends for?

Call your insurance agent. Inform him a garage sale is about to take place. If the current insurance does not cover the expected crowd, secure a temporary policy. The peace of mind is worth it.

Getting Out the Word

Spend your money on classified advertisements and signage. Use your mouth for the balance of the promotion. Classified advertising is inexpensive. Display advertising is expensive. If selling personal property from downsizing, you only need to advertise once. If selling the material from an estate, you may wish to place two classified advertisements, each separated by a week.

▼ TIP Do not list your name or telephone number in your classified advertisement.

You have enough to do. You do not want to be bothered by individuals asking permission to shop in advance or who have an endless array of questions. Curiosity is more than enough to drive people to your sale.

There are three types of signs that you need—presale tease, directional, and on-site. Do not be afraid to make your own signs.

Information That Belongs in Your Classified Advertisement

Date
Time
Address

BUZZWORDS SUCH AS:

Bargains galore
Contents of an estate or downsizing
Nothing held back
Everything priced to sell
Plenty of bargains
Everything ready for use

Do NOT waste money on providing directions. Garage sale shoppers all have local maps.

Most individuals do. These signs have a one-time use. They will be destroyed when you are finished with them.

About two to three weeks prior to the sale, place a sign at the location of the sale reading: "GARAGE SALE HERE / DAY / TIME / BARGAINS GALORE." This is all you need. Keep the sign simple.

Make simple signs that say "GARAGE SALE" and a directional arrow. Mark two to four main routes to the location of your sale the night before your sale begins. If there is not a convenient place to hang a sign, you need to provide one. Most people attach the directional sign to a wooden stake and drive it into the ground.

TIP Keep on-site signage minimal.

On-site signage includes signs explaining pricing codes if based on colored dots, identifying groupings, no smoking, parking restrictions, and location of cashier. Use a sign only if helpful.

Your best customers will be business acquaintances, church members, participants in clubs, civic, and service organizations, family, friends, and neighbors. Start touting the sale to them three to four weeks in advance. Consider developing a one-page flyer that you can post on the bulletin boards at churches, grocery stores, social halls, etc., and hand out to neighbors.

Immediately Before the Sale

Secure the required help. The ideal number of individuals is four, but if the sale is extremely large increase the number to six. If you do not have enough volunteers, hire the help you need.

TIP Use help that is loyal to you.

Think carefully about involving family and friends. The general rule of thumb is that those involved in the garage sale will not be shopping the sale. Garage sales are not the time or place to air family disputes. One person needs to be in charge. Anyone who is not prepared to give one-hundred-percent support to the person in charge should not be helping at the sale.

Cashier, floater, and security are the three basic garage sale positions. The cashier does the negotiating, totals the sale, collects the money due, and is responsible for the security of all money received. The floater moves throughout the garage sale answering questions, rearranges the merchandise when necessary to enhance salability, and changes sticker prices when the discount period starts. Security is a full-time job.

FACT A cardboard box does not constitute a secure cash box.

Make a trip to the bank and get ample change. Get twice the amount you think you will need. Also buy a metal cash box if you do not already own one.

Set up the sale one to two days in advance. People will stop and try to buy during setup. Say NO! If the sale is taking place outside, make certain you have the means to cover the objects at night. You also might want to consider having someone available to watch them as well.

FACT Seventy-five percent of the sales at a garage sale take place in the first three or four hours.

Keep an eye on the weather. The go or no go decision is generally made about 11 P.M. the night before the sale. Rain is the primary reason for canceling. If rain is called for in the morning but the afternoon is supposed to be clear, cancel the sale. If you do cancel, place a big sign on the yard announcing the new date.

If the night is clear and the weather report favorable, post the direction signs for the sale around 11 P.M. This will save you much needed time on the day of the sale.

TIP Go to bed around midnight and get a good night's rest.

The Sale

Start the garage sale at 7 A.M. You can select a later time, but the first shoppers will be knocking on the door at 7 A.M. Do not fight the inevitable. Start your garage sale at 7 A.M.

Get up at 5 A.M. If you did not put out your direction signs the night before, make it your first priority. In areas with high humidity it may make sense to wait until morning to put out the signs so they aren't ruined by dew. You want your signs to look fresh.

💎 | TIP | Start your sale on time.

Put the finishing touches on setting up your sale. Review the responsibilities of each person who will assist in the sale. Tell early shoppers that they have to wait until the official opening time.

The first two to three hours of any garage sale are the most hectic. Keep calm, but remember that you are in charge. The rules that govern the sale are the rules that you made. Stick to them. Do not allow yourself to be pushed. Deal with one person at a time. If the cashier is swamped, send a second person over to help by totaling the sale in advance or helping individuals pack their purchases.

💎 | FACT | Most garage sale customers prefer to pack their purchases themselves.

As a courtesy, have plenty of plastic bags and newspaper on hand. A couple dozen cardboard boxes also is a nice added feature. Title, that is, ownership of an object, changes hands when the bill is paid. Do not hesitate to ask customers to pack their purchases.

💎 | FACT | Everything is not going to sell in the first three hours even if you do believe in miracles.

There are many reasons why an object is not selling—the right buyer has not come along, no one appreciates it, it is out of fashion, etc. Forget this rationale. As far as you need be concerned, there is only one reason your objects are not selling—they are priced too high. If you are going to have any chance of selling them, you need to start reducing prices.

TIP If you priced your items to sell, you should be able to avoid deep discounting.

Consider reducing prices ten to twenty percent in the fourth hour, another ten to twenty percent in the fifth hour. Make up signs in advance reading "EVERYTHING DISCOUNTED _____ PERCENT." Discounting generally bottoms out at fifty percent of the initial asking price. However, in the last hour of the sale, put out a sign reading "NO REASONABLE OFFER REFUSED." Fifteen minutes before the sale ends, put out one final sign reading "IF YOU CAN USE IT, TAKE IT."

You may want to consider taking left bids on larger pieces or groupings, a sales practice used by the estate sale professional. When the sale is over, you need to contact the bidder. A change of heart and/or mind may have occurred in the interim. You set a date and time when the bidder comes to pay and pick up the object or objects. This does not always go smoothly. Often the buyer wants to haggle further. He knows the object did not sell. He has you at a distinct disadvantage.

TIP Think twice about taking sealed bids.

Tell those individuals who want to leave sealed bids that you have a discount policy and encourage them to return once price reductions have started. Tell them you will be happy to sell it to them at that time. You will be surprised. When given the option of buying now or losing an item, most garage sale shoppers will opt to buy the item now.

Garage sale buyers love to haggle. They cannot help themselves. If an object is priced at twenty-five cents, they will offer a dime. If it is priced at one dollar, they will offer fifty cents. You need to decide how much haggling you are willing to do. If you did your homework and set your prices slightly below what you saw similar items priced at other garage sales, you should not have to haggle.

FACT One of the hardest things to do is watch a potential customer walk away. Have courage, especially during the first three or four hours, and stay the course.

Over and over again, you will be asked: "Is this your best price?" "Can you do better?" or "Will you take 'x'?" Here are some responses to keep you in control of the selling situation:

1) No, it is not my best price. Actually my best price is higher, but since I wanted to sell this, I put this price on it.
2) Everyone can do better. Can you do better by paying the price I am asking?
3) It is early in the sale. I am going to hold firm on my prices for the first three (or four) hours. If you come back in the final hours of the sale, I do plan to reduce prices. Hopefully the item you want will still be here.
4) Thank you for your offer. I know you have thought carefully before making it. To be honest, I am willing to wait to see if someone comes along who wants this more than you do.
5) There has been a great deal of interest in this piece. At least a half a dozen individuals (okay, just maybe you are stretching the truth a bit) have looked at this piece. I am confident it is going to sell for the price I am asking.

TIP Make your help and yourself take an occasional break. Keep everyone fresh.

Do not plan to take a break until the early afternoon. Keep snacks such as energy bars on hand to get you through the morning. Keep snacks and drinks for your help and yourself in a separate location. You do not want to spill liquid on the objects you are trying to sell.

◆ | FACT | The bathroom in your home is not a public facility.

Do not allow any garage sale buyer to enter your house. Prior to the sale, note the location of the nearest public restrooms so you have a stock answer to the question, "I need a restroom. Can I use your bathroom?" Buyers are curious. They automatically assume there is more good stuff behind the closed doors. When someone asks you if you have more to sell, your stock answer should be: "What you see is what I have to sell."

Expect your sale to run a half hour to an hour longer than advertised. There are garage sale stragglers. Money is money.

However, every garage sale reaches a point where it should be shut down. Trust your instinct to know when that is. When that point is reached, end the sale.

Before you celebrate, clean up and secure any unsold objects. If you take a break, you are not likely to do the cleanup and securing until the next day. Remember, one of your goals is "over and done in a day." Done means done—nothing more to do, finished!

After the Sale

Make certain to remove any signs you placed. Do the accounting and deposit the proceeds.

If everything sold, you are one fortunate individual. The chances of this happening are slim. Almost everyone who conducts a garage sale has an assortment of objects that did not sell.

If someone approaches you during the sale and offers to buy anything you have left, make certain to get the person's name, address, and telephone number. Make arrangements for him to return an hour after the sale is concluded or first thing the following morning. If this option presents itself, by all means take it.

A single bulk sale is only one method to dispose of unsold and now unwanted objects. Additional options are explored in chapters twelve and thirteen.

Auctions, estate sales, and garage sales are not the only sale opportunities available to you if downsizing or settling an estate. Let's explore additional moneymaking opportunities before considering donation or sending objects to the landfill.

CHAPTER TEN

Additional Options for the Sale of Antiques, Collectibles, and Fine Arts

THE number of antiques, collectibles, and fine arts objects you own may be too small to attract the interest of an auctioneer. An estate sale may not be the right venue to maximize their value. Antiques, collectibles, and fine art objects (with the possible exception of more recent collectibles from the late 1960s and 1970s, as discussed in chapter nine) definitely do not belong in a garage sale.

Auction and estate sales are the most frequently used methods for the sale of antiques, collectibles, and fine art objects. However, other choices exist. Alternatives include direct sale, antiques malls, and flea markets. Each has its advantages and disadvantages.

All these sales methods have one thing in common—a commitment of time and energy from you. Just as in a garage sale, you need to be proactive in the sales process if you want to maximize your return.

Direct Sale

Direct sales are private sales, either to individual collectors or to dealers. Direct sale is an alternative for those individuals who do not want their possessions or the items in an estate exposed to the general public. "I do not want anyone to know my private business" still is a prevalent mind-set.

Direct sales, like garage sales, generally involve cash. Auctions and estate sales leave a paper trail. Once again it must be noted that legally capital gains must be reported on all sales of personal property. But if your goal is immediate cash-in-hand, direct sales can be a good option.

Identifying the right buyer or buyers is the key to selling direct. While it would be ideal if that buyer were local, chances are he is not. As a result the buyer has to factor into any price he is willing to pay the cost of his time, transportation to meet the seller to inspect the items for sale, meals, lodging, and shipping to relocate the items from the seller's location to his location.

Direct sale works best when the antiques, collectibles, and fine arts are high-end and upper-middle-market objects. Lower-middle-market and commonly found objects, the vast majority of antiques, collectibles, and fine arts, are better sold at auction or an estate sale.

Dealer

A single dealer generally does not have the finances to buy a large collection (see chapter five). If the number of pieces is small, for example, fifty or fewer, a dealer is a viable sales option.

A dealer expects to buy at wholesale. You as the seller may feel that if a dealer doubles the amount he pays, this is a fair profit. Actually a dealer needs to triple the price he pays if he wants to be successful. At my Institute for the Study of Antiques and Collectibles, dealers are taught: "Double your money, pay your expenses. Triple your money, pay yourself." No one likes working for free. Dealers are no exception.

FACT A specialist dealer will pay more than a generalist dealer.

Dealers specialize. If the antique, collectible, and fine art objects selected for disposal are from more than one collecting category, you will need to involve multiple specialized dealers. It may be necessary for you to interact with more than one dealer in each specialty. It would be nice to assume the first person through the door will buy everything you have to offer. Wish it, but do not count on it.

TIP When selling direct, patience is indeed a virtue.

Dealers are busy individuals. They book commitments, such as antiques shows, six months to a year in advance. They cannot always come at your beck and call. Arranging a convenient time for a dealer to inspect the material you have for sale may take from several weeks to several months.

Before inviting a dealer to visit and inspect the objects you wish to sell, you must decide if the sale is take-it-all or pick-and-choose. A dealer has a right to know this prior to a visit. Dealers prefer to pick and choose, obviously a choice that works more to their advantage than the seller's.

Dealers buy with customers in mind. In buying any group of objects, they want to see enough sales potential to recover the money they spend within two to four weeks, double their investment in four to eight weeks, and be able to sell everything they buy in six months. Some dealers work on an even more accelerated time schedule.

FACT Dealers know what they can and cannot sell.

Dealers are very reluctant to buy pieces that they know will remain in inventory for a very long time in order to obtain the pieces they want. They may consider doing this when the number of undesirable pieces is small. However, if the less desirable items make up more than twenty-five percent of what you are selling, they are more likely to walk away.

A dealer who sold the highest percentage of the objects now being offered for sale to the person downsizing or deceased is the first dealer who should be contacted about buying the objects. Although the degree of collector-dealer loyalty in the twenty-first century has diminished, contacting this dealer still makes sense. The dealer knows the collection, perhaps better than the person selling it. His knowledge of what he sold allows him to ask about pieces that might have been overlooked.

Collector's club membership lists are a great source for identifying potential dealers and private collector buyers. Once again, check David Maloney Jr.'s *Maloney's Antiques & Collectibles Resource Directory.*

Before inviting a dealer to view the objects you have for sale, check his professional reputation. If the dealer sets up in the antiques show circuit, ask him to provide you with the names and contact information for several show promoters. If he has a shop or sells privately, ask for a résumé. Don't bother to check with other dealers. Professional courtesy dictates that one dealer never disparages another.

Is this necessary? The answer is yes, if for no other reason than your own peace of mind.

FACT You are obligated to set the price on the items you wish to sell.

Do not call in a dealer expecting him to make an offer. This is tantamount to providing a free appraisal. Dealers are professionals. They know when they are being played off against one another.

While the one sealed bid sale method discussed in chapter five is a viable approach, it is not recommended in this situation unless the number of items exceeds fifty. Direct sale means what the term implies, the immediate direct sale of the objects.

FACT Nothing leaves without complete payment.

If the final purchase price is large, a dealer may request that he be allowed to pay in several installments. This is fine provided you retain everything purchased until the final payment is made. Refuse to allow the dealer to take some of the objects. When such a request is made, the dealer is most likely trying to sell these objects to raise the money to make subsequent payments. If this does not happen, the dealer may simply not pay the balance owed. Better to lose a little rather than a lot is his philosophy. Further, the first objects removed are usually the best objects. Once a dealer has cherry-picked the collection for what he wants, he may feel no obligation to go back for the rest.

FACT Most direct sales are based on a handshake rather than a written contract.

Since most direct sales involve cash, no written contract is used. In most instances the only people present when the deal is done are the buyer and seller. When there are no witnesses, truth becomes one person's word against the other's.

Make certain that at least you have a witness present when selling direct. Suggest to the buyer that he do the same. If concerned, write a brief sales agreement and make certain each party signs it.

Title passes when the money changes hands. If a buyer asks you to retain possession of objects he has purchased until he can come and pick them up, carefully consider this before saying yes. Normally in a direct purchase, the buyer is expected to take the objects he purchased with him when he leaves. If you retain them, who is responsible if an object is stolen or damaged? What happens if the buyer does not return as promptly as he promised? It is best to avoid these and any other problems. Make it clear to the buyer before he visits that you expect him to take his purchases with him the day of the purchase.

Private Collector

Many of the same issues and concerns involved in selling direct to a dealer also apply to selling direct to a private collector. However there are some key differences.

A private collector is going to be far more selective in what he is willing to buy. Most private collectors are seeking pieces they need to complete their collections. They have little interest in purchasing duplicates. Assuming they will buy duplicates for trading purposes is a mistake. The amount of trading among collectors is greatly overestimated. Most collectors do not trade.

Of course there are collector-dealers, those individuals who sell to support their collecting habit. They always are looking for fresh inventory. Because they sell primarily in the specialized show circuit, their focus is on middle and high-end market pieces. They have no interest in commonly found objects.

FACT Today the private collector expects to be treated like a dealer when buying privately.

The long-standing assumption is that private collectors will pay more for an object than a dealer. Assuming the private collector wanted and needed the object, the basic rule was that a private collector would pay around seventy percent of full market retail.

This is no longer true. Today's private collectors are much more sophisticated. Realizing they are competing on the direct sale circuit with dealers, they expect to be treated like dealers. At best private collectors will now pay five to ten percent above dealer price. An object would have to be exceptional for a private collector to pay a premium.

● | TIP | There are no friends in a buying transaction.

If the person downsizing is a collector, he already knows the private collectors he needs to contact. They are his friends and rivals. If he expects them to pay a premium because of this, he is mistaken. In fact, the seller may find them a tougher audience because they are aware of the seller's need to sell.

If the executor of an estate, do not be surprised at the number of inquiries you will receive from private collectors in the weeks and months following the death of the deceased. Collectors know each others' collections. When a collector dies, even if the collection is not large, collectors circle like vultures. Many private collectors will offer to help an unknowledgeable collector. All have one basic motive in mind—get inside before anyone else does.

Once again collectors' club membership lists and *Maloney's Antiques & Collectibles Resource Directory* are excellent sources for the name and address information for private collectors. The deceased's address book and/or phone file is another.

● | FACT | You are under no obligation to tell a buyer who else has been invited to the table.

Whom you invite to buy direct is your private business. Expect potential buyers to pressure you for this information. Everyone in the antiques, collectibles, and fine arts business knows everyone else. Buyers also will pressure you to tell them where on the list of buyers they are located, for example, first, second, third, etc. Once again, this is none of their business. If they pressure you on any of the above points, a quick response of "if you are that concerned,

I will be happy to remove your name from the list I have prepared" should suffice.

♦ TIP Do not allow yourself to be intimidated by a person who has more expertise than you.

Dealers and private buyers often try to use their knowledge to intimidate a seller. Their goal is simple. They want to be in charge of the buying situation.

The techniques dealers and private collectors use to achieve this end are many. They will make disparaging remarks about an object, for example, by pointing out every wear mark or flaw, in hope of lowering its apparent value in the eye of the seller. They will use their extensive knowledge of the history of the material and trade to increase the seller's trust in them, expecting the seller to believe that whatever they say has to be true.

Hiring a skilled collection dispersal manager, one who is as familiar with the category and trade as the potential buyer, to handle sale negotiations levels the playing field. The extra money made will more than cover the professional's compensation. This professional is your representative and ethically cannot be a purchaser. Some appraisers also offer this service. Once again, *Maloney's Antiques & Collectibles Resource Directory* is an excellent resource for locating such individuals.

Trade Periodicals

When selling a top-end antique, collectible, or fine art object directly, consider placing a display advertisement in one or more antiques and collectibles trade periodicals. A list of general trade periodicals is found in Appendix II. Specialized trade periodicals are found in *Maloney's Antiques & Collectibles Resource Directory*.

Pictures sell antiques, collectibles, and fine art objects far better than words. Although most trade papers still offer classified advertising, a display advertisement picturing the object is preferable.

A full- or half-page display advertisement is not required. A sixteenth or eighth of a page advertisement usually is more than sufficient to do the job.

Rates vary. Most trade periodicals include a rate chart on or near the page that lists the paper's staff. Do not place a display advertisement unless you are convinced you can recover the advertisement's full cost and more above the price you initially hoped to receive.

TIP Avoid the temptation to include a price followed by "or best offer" in a display advertisement.

Once you have selected the periodical or periodicals in which you wish to advertise, check to see if display advertisements normally include the price asked. Even if this is not standard practice, consider doing it. Indicating the asking price limits contact to serious buyers.

Dealers and private collectors strongly resist any buying situation that turns into a two- to five-party private auction. "Or best offer" opens the door to this possibility. Further, while the seller feels this will encourage individuals to offer more, just the opposite is true. Most "best offers" will be below the asking price. Buyers interpret "or best offer" as an invitation to negotiate.

Private and Charitable Institutions

Most institutions encourage individuals to donate objects. They cite nonexistent or very limited acquisition budgets.

The simple truth is that many private and charitable institutions buy direct. If they want to acquire an object badly enough, they have means of finding the money to purchase it. If they do not have the funds in-house, they can approach a member of their board or another donor to fund the acquisition. Many institutions sell objects that no longer fit the museum's mission statement to obtain funds to purchase those items that do.

Museums Do Buy Items: A Case Study

A man who was renovating a building found a large collection of records relating to the Lehigh Coal and Navigation Company. He called a local museum and told them about his find. The museum immediately asked if he would consider donating the collection.

As anyone who has done renovation knows, it is an expensive proposition. As much as this man would have liked to donate the collection, his financial needs had to come first.

He called in an expert to examine the collection and supervise its sale. The expert had both object valuation knowledge and a museum background. A myriad of sale options were discussed including offering the collection to the museum on a right of first refusal basis.

Although realizing the amount received would have been far greater had the collection been sold piecemeal, the owner decided to give the museum the right of first refusal. The owner and his consultant established a price.

The museum was invited to inspect the collection. A curator from the museum was on the inspection committee, confident that he could pressure the owner into gifting rather than selling the material. Upon arriving and seeing the consultant rather than the owner, he realized his goal was untenable.

In the end the museum purchased the collection for the asking price. The museum realized that the asking price was less than half the fair market value of the objects. The chance to acquire the entire collection as a unit was too good to pass up.

After acquiring the collection, the museum issued an appeal letter to its members asking them to help pay for the acquisition.

FACT The best deals are made when both parties speak the same language.

If you have an object or group of objects that you know fit into the collection scope of a private or charitable institution, offer them to the institution. Once again consider engaging the services of a professional with collection management experience to assist you. A sale goes smoother when both parties are equally knowledgeable.

Antiques Mall

An antiques mall is an inexpensive sales method to expose a limited amount of antiques, collectibles, and fine arts object to a small, but select buying public in a relatively short period of time. Most of the sellers in an antiques mall are part-time dealers. Do not be dismayed by this. An antiques mall serves the short-time seller as well.

Visit the local antiques malls within a one-hundred-mile radius. During your visit study the type of merchandise being sold at the mall and prices asked, observe the mall's cleanliness and the helpfulness of the staff, and talk with the manager about rental terms, where the mall is advertised, security, and payment.

TIP The best antiques mall for you may be located several states away.

If your antiques, collectibles, and fine arts objects sell better in one region than another, you need to offer them for sale in the region in which they will do best. Look for a large antiques mall featuring a combination of booths and cases located within a few minutes' drive of a heavily trafficked Interstate exit.

Resolve to limit your antique sales experience to no more than four months. Three months is preferable. If you priced the objects to sell, three months should be more than sufficient.

Resist the Temptation to Become a Dealer

Whether downsizing or the sole heir to a large estate, you are far better off with the money from the sale of the objects you do not want to keep than using this material as the inventory basis to establish yourself as an antiques dealer.

Dealing in antiques, collectibles, and/or fine art objects requires a great deal of time, education, and effort, even when done on a part-time basis. The overhead is tremendous. If the amount of time is factored against profits, many individuals who sell antiques work for close to or under minimum wage.

If you want to become an antiques dealer, first, educate yourself, second, develop a firm business plan, and, third, do not give up your day job.

Because you plan to be in the antiques mall for a relatively short period of time, consider renting cases rather than a booth to display your merchandise. Avoid the overhead costs involved in acquiring display furniture or decorating the booth. If you have items that are too large for a case, ask the antiques mall manager if you can place the objects on consignment or rent by the square foot in a general display area.

TIP Fully understand all fees involved before signing a contract.

Do not rent space in an antiques mall without a contract. Most antiques malls will ask you to sign a six-month or full-year contract. Do not be intimidated by this request. Many antiques malls will rent on a month-to-month basis if they have space available. After all, any tenant is better than no tenant.

A per-case fee is common practice. Some malls actually rent on a shelf-by-shelf basis. If you rent a booth, rent is based on square footage. However, the rent is often only the first of many charges you will encounter.

Most, but not all, malls charge a percentage of sales. This percentage can range from six to fifteen percent. Some malls assess a special monthly fee to help defray the costs of advertisement, pass along the cost of credit card sales to their renters, and/or require renters to work a specific number of hours per week or month or pay for a substitute.

Price the objects you plan to sell in the mall below those found on similar objects. Antiques malls are very competitive sales environments. Do not fall victim to the helpful seller or mall manager who says, "You have that priced far too low. You can do much better." Your stock response is: "I am glad you think so. I will be happy to sell it to you and let you make the extra profit you are certain is in it."

Antiques mall buyers are comparison shoppers. Most have a good idea of the price they want to pay. All are eager buyers when they find something they want at bargain prices.

The standard pricing rule for antiques mall merchandise is twenty to twenty-five percent above wholesale. The theory is to challenge the dealers' view of value and provide bargain prices in the eyes of the general public.

Your goal is to sell your objects. You do not care who buys them as long as they sell. Consider offering your objects at wholesale or at a price as close to wholesale with which you are comfortable. Further, return to the mall and reduce the price at the end of the second month.

TIP Do not sell an object in an antiques mall that you cannot afford to lose.

Theft is a major problem at antiques malls. Mall managers and owners know this and work hard to prevent it. Do not be surprised if it happens to you. If you are overly concerned, secure a temporary policy from the Antiques and Collectibles Dealers Association, part of the Antiques and Collectibles Associations groups. Their address appears earlier in this book. You also can find out more details by clicking on the logo found on my Web site, *harryrinker.com.*

Recently several antiques malls have been the victims of fire and natural disasters such as hurricanes. Sellers in the mall discovered that while the mall owner's insurance policy covered the building and equipment owned by the mall company, it did not cover the merchandise of the sellers. Most antiques mall contracts clearly note it is the responsibility of the seller to provide his own insurance coverage against loss, damage, and theft.

TIP Create the appearance that your merchandise is selling.

Visit the antiques mall every two to three weeks to rearrange the merchandise in your case or cases. As merchandise sells, reduce the amount of space you rent. The simple act of rearranging merchandise may be sufficient to sell it. If you do not have the time or inclination to do this, ask the antiques mall owner or manager if you can pay someone to do this for you.

Flea Market

There are many types of flea markets, thus making the term difficult to define. If you visit the Rose Bowl Flea Market in Pasadena, California, you will find discontinued and knock-off merchandise, crafts, clothing (from tube socks to dresses), home-care products, plants of all types, and specialty foods as much in evidence as antiques and collectibles. On the other hand, if you visit the Ann Arbor Antiques Market in Michigan, you will find primarily middle- and high-end antiques, collectibles, and fine arts objects.

While most flea markets occur at regular intervals, the interval can be weekly, bimonthly, monthly, or seasonal. Many flea markets now feature extravaganza weekends, a market at which additional dealers often expand the flea market's size by two to three times.

Antiques, Collectibles, and Fine Arts Objects

If you plan to sell antiques, collectibles, and fine art objects, you want to find a flea market that is devoted to this type of material. They are most easily identified through advertisements in antique trade periodicals. Scan six months' worth of papers before identifying the flea market at which you wish to sell.

If possible visit the flea market at which you are planning to sell. If time is a consideration, call the manager and ask him to answer any questions you have about selling at his flea market.

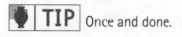 Once and done.

Plan to sell everything in one visit. Your goal is to get rid of things, not haul them home. Once again how you price your objects is critical to achieving your goal. Just as with an antiques mall, it pays to visit flea markets in the area where you are planning to sell and noting prices. Because you plan to be in and out in one setup, your prices need to be below those normally found there.

Most antiques and collectibles flea markets are two days in length. A few have a setup day with an early-buyer feature prior to the market opening to the general public. This means that you have the added sale expenses of another day's lodging and meals.

Many antiques and collectibles flea markets feature outdoor as well as indoor rental space. Indoor space rents at a premium. Since you only plan to sell once, rent indoor space if possible. Indoor space at most antiques and collectibles flea markets is limited and reserved for regulars.

Basic Equipment Needed to
Set Up at a Flea Market

Extra tables in case the ones provided are not sturdy

Table coverings

Plastic covers for tables in case of rain

Clips to hold covers in place in case of wind and rain

Chairs for you and your assistant

Umbrella to shade you and your assistant if not using a tent

Hat

Signage

Tags for pricing

Flash and/or flood light—some flea markets set up beginning at 5 A.M.

Cash box

Plenty of change, especially one- and five-dollar bills

Testing kit for fifty- and hundred-dollar bills

Sales receipt book

Pens/pencils

Ice chest loaded with water, soda, or whatever

Snacks

Feather duster and clean rags

Toilet paper and hand wipes—backup just in case the Johnny on the Spot toilets are not adequately equipped

TIP If there is the slightest chance of rain, do not sell at a flea market.

If you are forced to sell outside, you need rain protection. You most likely need protection from the sun as well. If you have or can borrow a tent, you are in good shape. If not, tent rental is an added selling expense.

Flea markets are subject to the elements. Winds blow. Fine dust is a given. It is not the environment for someone who likes things prim and proper.

Most antiques and collectibles flea markets include two to three tables as part of the rental package. The seller is expected to provide everything else. Unless you already own most of the material you need, think twice about incurring the expenses to acquire it. No flea markets of which I am aware provide rental equipment.

Do not attempt to sell at a flea market alone. If you have to use the facilities, you need someone to cover your booth. Your booth neighbor is not the answer. A second person is essential, if for no other reason than to provide security.

FACT Price haggling is expected at a flea market.

Even if you price the objects you wish to sell below standard prices seen at the flea market, buyers still will haggle. Expect to reduce your items an additional five to ten percent if you want to close the sale.

As a one-time seller, limit your merchandise to smalls, that is, objects that fit on the top of a table. Once again, you want to avoid the unnecessary expense of buying display shelving.

TIP You can sell from photographs. It is not easy, but you can do it.

If you have larger piece, you can try selling them from photographs. Put together a book of photographs. Price the objects. Note on the cover of the book that these objects are available for sale on an "appointment" basis.

Many of the same principles that apply to running a garage sale also apply to selling at an antiques and collectibles flea market. If you decide to use this sales method, read or reread the preceding chapter.

Swap Meet

A swap meet is a flea market where the primary value of the merchandise is reuse or discounted. It is not the place you want to sell antique, collectible, and fine art objects.

However, if you have a large quantity of reusable goods and do not sell them via auction or garage sale, consider setting up for a day at a local swap meet. Swap meets are another recycling venue.

Most swap meets are outdoors and last two days. While some feature booths, most have long rows of tables separated by aisles for the customers. Rent is on a per-table basis.

Swap meet buyers expect to buy things cheap. Garage sale merchandise fits the bill. Most swap meet buyers are looking for things they can use on an everyday basis.

Boxes filled with items and marked "Your Choice 25¢" to "Your Choice $2.00" are extremely popular. Five dollars for any object is considered a great deal of money. Once again, assuming you price your items to sell you should be able to leave a swap meet with an extra two to three hundred dollars in your pocket.

One Final Option: Consignment Shop

While consignment is a risky approach to selling a collection (see chapter five), it is a viable approach when the number of antiques, collectibles, and fine art objects is small in number. Consignment increases the probability that the right buyer will discover an object and pay a premium price.

Most communities have one or more "white elephant" or other form of consignment/recycling shops. Some antiques shops feature a consignment corner or room. Middle-level antiques, collectibles, and fine art objects are the items that sell best in the consignment shop environment. It is best to sell high-end pieces at auction or privately. Commonly found examples are a tough sell in any sales venue.

TIP Never consign without a contract, and read its terms carefully.

Do not place items on consignment without a contract. Read the contract carefully. The contract should contain provisions that protect the rights of the seller and consignor. If it is weighted heavily toward the rights of the seller, think twice before signing.

A consignment shop charges between thirty-five and forty percent of the selling price if it is allowed to set the asking price. If the consignor insists on setting the asking price, a five- to ten-percent penalty is added.

The traditional consignment period is four to six months. Insist on three if you can. If the consignment shop is unsuccessful in selling your object or objects, you want to get them back as soon as possible to try them in another venue.

Most consignment shops have a policy of reducing the asking price on a weekly or bimonthly basis. Make certain you agree with the store's policy before signing the contract. In the third month the reduction can be as much as fifty percent of the initial asking price.

Once you place an object on consignment, it cannot be removed without paying a penalty. This protects the consignor as well as you. If you talk about an object on consignment with someone and he expresses an interest in buying it, either send him to the consignment shop or ask him to wait until your consignment agreement expires. If he decides to do the latter, he needs to understand that the object might be sold before that date, at which point he is simply out of luck.

TIP Know who is responsible if an object is broken or stolen.

Most household insurance policies continue to provide coverage for objects on consignment. The object belongs to the seller, not the consignment shop. However you should not assume this is the case for your policy—better to contact your insurance agent and ask.

If you do not want everyone in your local community to know that you are selling items, then consign your objects to a shop located several hundred miles away. There is no anonymity in a local community. Someone is bound to recognize one or more of your objects. The word will spread quickly. Understand the positive side of this situation. If well known in the community, your name associated with an object gives it a personal touch and can assist in its sale.

TIP Your objects will not get sold faster if you visit the consignment shop to ask how sales are progressing.

Let the consignment shop professionals do their job. There is no need for you to personally visit the pieces on a regular basis. If you miss them this much, you probably should not have considered selling them.

Insist on an accounting twice a month, once a month at the very least. Asking the consignment shop to put a check in the mail every time an object is sold is unreasonable.

If objects remain at the end of the consignment period, make arrangements to have them picked up as soon as possible. Although the consignment shop owner may plead with you to renew the contract, the simple truth is that the shop was not able to sell your pieces. It is time to move forward, not backward.

Did You Notice?

If you have not been aware of it before now, the chapters dealing with the sale of objects have moved progressively from the sales method involving the least amount of personal involvement to the methods involving the largest amount of personal involvement.

The Internet, the one sale method yet to be discussed, requires the greatest personal involvement in the sales process in respect to the seller's time. Read on.

CHAPTER ELEVEN

Selling on the Internet

THE Internet, that is, the World Wide Web, is infinite. Today's marketplace is global. The Internet has expanded the buyer-seller community many fold.

The Internet and eBay are not synonymous. There are other auction Web sites, for example, Overstock and Yahoo. There are storefront Web sites, for example, Go Antiques, Ruby Lane, and TIAS, that contain hundreds of "stores" selling antiques and collectibles. Many auction companies and private sellers have their own Web sites. The Internet is the modern frontier for business entrepreneurship.

> **FACT** You are not going into business. You are looking to get in and get out of the internet marketplace in as short a time as possible.

Having stated this, assume for the purposes of this book that the Internet and eBay are synonymous. Like the title song to the television show *Cheers* suggests, "You want to go where everybody knows your name." EBay is king of the hill. Long live the king!

EBay thinks of itself as a nation of buyers and sellers. If true, it is the fifth largest nation in the world. Only China, India, the United States, and Indonesia are larger. EBay is a global entity.

Most Americans are familiar with eBay.com. EBay.com is only

the American eBay Web site. EBay is much bigger. Check out the bottom left corner of the home page of eBay.com. There are eBay sites listed for twenty-six other nations—Argentina, Australia, Austria, Belgium, Brazil, Canada, China, France, Germany, Hong Kong, India, Ireland, Italy, Korea, Malaysia, Mexico, the Netherlands, New Zealand, the Philippines, Poland, Singapore, Spain, Sweden, Switzerland, Taiwan, and the United Kingdom. This list will grow as eBay continues its global expansion.

FACT At the moment, no states with state auctioneer licensing laws are enforcing these laws with respect to individuals conducting auctions solely on the Internet.

EBay is an auction platform. Essentially eBay allows you to become a part-time auctioneer. However, unlike a standard auction that continues until the last bidder is active, an eBay auction ends at a specific moment. Whoever is the high bidder at that point wins the auction. If there were individuals who would have continued to bid higher, they are out of luck.

EBay also offers storefront, that is, direct sale, opportunities. Individuals planning to become regular sellers on eBay should explore them. If you are liquidating objects from downsizing or an estate, your involvement on eBay will be temporary. You want to end your selling experience in the shortest time possible.

FACT Most of the items sold on eBay go to end users.

EBay has an established reputation for getting the best price. While true to a large degree, there are plenty of exceptions. EBay's price strength rests on the fact that most of its buyers are end users. They are not buying the item for resale but to use. In theory they are prepared to pay the highest price. In reality eBay buyers are looking for bargains just like everyone else.

Do You Have the Time to Invest?

Selling on the Internet takes time, a great deal of time. Each object has to be researched so an adequate description can be written and it must be photographed for the listing. Once a listing is posted, the seller has to be available to answer questions. When the auction is concluded, the winner has to be contacted and payment collected. When payment is received, the object has to be packed and shipped. The sale concludes when the buyer receives the package and indicates satisfaction.

Ideally you want to list between twenty and thirty objects each day. While this may not present a problem at the beginning of your selling experience, it will as the selling experience proceeds. As auctions close, you need to attend to the details involved in completing the transaction. Plan to devote half a day to this at least.

Look at the piles of objects you want to sell. How many objects are there? Divide the number by twenty. Think conservatively. This will provide you with an approximation of the number of days you will need for researching and listing. A realistic look at this number may well force you to conclude that some of the other sale options are far more attractive.

TIP Do you have the patience and persistence to sell on eBay?

Realistically you probably will need several months to sell your objects on eBay. Not all your objects will sell the first time. A sell-through rate of eighty percent is considered spectacular. Some objects may have to be listed several times. Some may never sell.

If you do plan to sell on the Internet, you need space to conduct the selling operation. If you are downsizing, you need to start the selling process three to four months before any scheduled move. If you do this, you can use your home. If you are the executor of an estate, you most likely will have to move the items you are planning to sell on the Internet to another location in order to make the real estate available for sale. If you have to rent space on a temporary basis, look closely at the potential income the objects represent and ask if this justifies the expense.

Equipment Needed and Its Use

You already may own most of the equipment you need to sell on eBay. Hardware consists of a computer and digital camera. A word-processing program and a photo editing program are the minimal software. Internet access and photo storage allow you to work on the Web. If you have none of the above, expect to spend between a thousand and two thousand dollars to acquire the bare necessities.

If the computer you own is more than five years old, check its working memory (RAM) and hard drive storage capacity. You may want to consider upgrading them. You are about to spend a great deal of time on your computer. Speed is important.

If you have to purchase a computer, consider buying a reconditioned laptop rather than a desktop model. You do not need a computer with the latest bells and whistles. The tasks you need to perform are extremely basic. A laptop is nice because you can move it around as you list objects rather than having to move objects from one location to a central work area and then back again. A laptop computer gives you the greatest flexibility.

FACT EBay buyers are frustrated by out-of-focus and poorly cropped pictures. Busy backgrounds also are not appreciated.

Pictures are critical to selling on eBay. Most digital cameras do not have the ability to do close-up photographs and keep in focus. If you do not have a camera that can photograph the mark on the bottom of a piece clearly, you need to purchase a camera that can.

Do not spend extra money to increase picture storage. Most likely you will be downloading your pictures directly into your computer.

Set aside an area and create a small photo studio. Photograph the object with a solid background behind it. Use a white or blue backdrop. An ironed sheet works just fine. Avoid photographing an object on a table in the middle of a room or outdoors. The busy background makes it hard to focus on the object.

There is no rule that says you have to limit your photographic presentation to one image. Use as many images as necessary to give the potential bidder all the essential information needed.

| TIP | Do not post an image until it satisfies you.

Light the object carefully. If you use the camera flash, there most likely will be a big bright spot in the middle of the object. Potential bidders find this especially annoying. You want to turn on bidders, not turn them off.

Any word-processing program is fine. If you are starting fresh, consider purchasing Microsoft Word. It is the industry standard, is easy to learn, and help from friends and others who use it is readily available.

| FACT | Photo editing is time-consuming. Limit it as much as possible.

Most digital cameras come with their own photo-editing software. If you photograph your objects correctly, little to no editing will be required. The software accompanying the camera will be more than sufficient.

If you plan to purchase photo-editing software, think Adobe Photoshop. Adobe Photoshop, like Microsoft Word, is the industry's standard.

You need access to the Internet. Your options are threefold—dial-up, high-speed, and wireless. The options open to you depend heavily on where you live. In some parts of the country, dial up is the only Internet access option. If possible choose wireless, albeit with the understanding that high-speed access is often much faster than wireless. If you are using a laptop computer, wireless provides maximum flexibility.

Most connection packages provide a limited amount of photographic storage. The same is true for eBay. If you decide to store the photographs on your computer, you need to leave your computer connected to the Internet twenty-four hours a day if you want your photographs to appear each time someone checks your listings. This is not desirable.

TIP Condense your images so they upload faster.

Many individuals take very high-resolution pictures. While clearer and sharper, these take longer to upload. Consider condensing your images to shorten the upload process.

How to Sell on eBay

There is absolutely no need to reinvent the wheel. There are dozens of books that explain how to sell on eBay. Here are three favorites:

Griffith, Jim "Griff." *The Official eBay Bible*. Gotham Books, 2003.
Miller, Michael. *The Absolute Beginner's Guide to eBay*, 3rd ed. Que, 2005.
Wiggins, Pamela. *Buying & Selling Antiques and Collectibles on eBay*. Thomson, 2004.

Honestly, you do not need any of these books. Across the top of eBay's home page, you will see a line of boxes that read: "Buy / Sell / My eBay / Community / Help." Click on "Sell." It will take you to a page with headings that include "Decide What to Sell," "Prepare to Sell,"

"List Your Item," and "Complete the Sale." Each of these headings contains a minitutorial.

TIP Print out the eBay tutorials.

EBay's tutorials cover a wide range of material. They are designed to help the individual who is selling a car as well as household goods, antiques, collectibles, and/or fine art objects. Cull out the information that applies to you. Print out the tutorials and put them in a binder, thus creating your own how-to book.

Importance of Item Title

Individuals wishing to buy the items identical to those you are offering for sale have to find them. Most will use the "search" feature on the home page rather than clicking on "advanced search." Even those using the "advanced search" feature do not always check the "search title and description" block.

Your choice of the words included in your item title line determines the ease by which potential buyers will find your items. Choosing the correct words requires careful thought.

One of the hardest things for sellers who are new to eBay to understand is that the words in the item title line do not have to make sense. What they have to be are the right words.

Think of the title line as a string of words consisting of the primary words a person would use to find your item. Each word is a bullet. This is not the place for phrases or complete sentences.

If you have a 1950s Hopalong Cassidy black-and-white school bag, your first inclination is to list it as a "1950s Hopalong Cassidy black-and-white school bag." The only problem is that no one searches by date or color. The date and color information belongs in the text. A far better bullet approach would be: "Hopalong Cassidy, Hoppy, School Bag, Book Bag, Briefcase, Satchel." Think nouns and not adjectives.

Besides date and color, information about scarcity, condition, and sale terms also belong in the description and not the item title. No one is going to do a search for "No Reserve."

I just did an advanced search with search title and description for "rare" and 1,002,539 listings appeared. No one is going to search through these. Likewise I did the same search for "scarce" and 42,582 listings appeared. Using these terms in the item title is a waste of space.

Read and reread the eBay.com Fees pages. Like most antiques malls, eBay's fees include a percentage of the final value obtained. The insertion (listing) and final value fees are the basic fees. Additional charges are levied if you place a reserve (a price below which the object will not sell) and the object does not sell, take advantage of the Buy It Now feature, upgrade the appearance of your listing, and insert additional pictures. Make certain you fully understand how charges are assessed before starting to sell.

EBay also offers a program known as eBay University. Go to eBay.com and type "eBay University" in the search block. EBay conducts classes in the field and online. Education Specialists trained by eBay also conduct classes locally, usually as part of an adult education program at a high school, college, or university. Watch for advertisements in your local newspaper

Think twice before responding to any direct e-mail solicitation to learn how to sell on eBay. As you already discovered, there are far better methods to obtain the information needed.

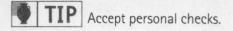 **TIP** Accept personal checks.

Do not make eBay payments difficult by limiting payments to credit cards or money orders. Be flexible. Take personal checks. The risk is minimal.

When selling on the Internet, individuals pay for their purchases before they receive them. There is a clear understanding that a seller will not release an item until the check used to pay for that item clears the bank.

Further, eBay's feedback system serves as a credit reference. If you are selling to a relatively new buyer, one with under fifty feedbacks, you may want to inquire if the person is willing to consider paying by credit card or money order to expedite the selling process. If the answer is no, accept the person's personal check and wait until it clears.

PayPal, just one of many credit card businesses serving Internet buyers and sellers, is part of the eBay empire. Since you have chosen to use the eBay platform, take advantage of its full range of services.

What Sells Well on eBay

The easiest way to check what sells well on eBay is to check eBay's "Completed Auctions." Once you have opened an eBay account, you have access to this information.

When checking prices realized, pay close attention to the information in the title line and listing. Use the format from successful auctions as a model for your listings.

TIP The real value is indicated by the price at which the third highest bidder withdrew from the bidding.

Check on the number of bidders. A low bid count indicates that interest may be minimal, usually due to a flooded market. Not every bid represents a different person. The bid count indicates the number of bid jumps. If a bidder bids more than once, each of his bids is indicated as a separate bid.

Also open the bid record. Look at the third highest bid. Notice the value difference between the second and third highest bids. If the interval is small, this suggests demand is strong. If the interval is great, then demand is low. Why the third bid? Think for a moment. Remove the winning bidder from the mix. A second example of the object appears at auction. The second highest bidder will not have to pay the amount of his earlier bid to buy it, but rather only one bid increment above what the third-highest bidder was willing to pay.

For this reason one needs to track eBay prices over a four-month period or longer to obtain a true understanding of an object's worth. Fortunately there are services that offer this information. EBay's home page provides access to ninety days' worth of data through its "Marketplace Research." Andale.com and GoAntiques.com's Price-Miner, accessed by clicking on "Price Guide" on its home page, offer similar services. Both charge a fee. PriceMiner includes prices realized from other auctions in addition to eBay.

FACT Some things sell better on eBay than others.

High-end objects, especially in post-1945 collecting categories, generally sell well on eBay. Paper items with decorative and local value also do well. EBay has strengthened the value of many local and regional objects. Utilitarian household objects in like-new condition often do better on eBay than at garage sales.

Objects that were marketed and are collected globally attract strong bidding. Hot-button topics include vintage clothing, movie, music, television memorabilia, and toys. Foreign buyers are active on eBay.com. Thanks to PayPal, payment problems such as international currency exchange, associated with selling to foreign buyers, have largely been eliminated. EBay also is working with postal services worldwide to reduce shipping costs.

What Sells Poorly on eBay

EBay showed the world that the survival rate of items was far higher than anyone suspected. Objects that many collectors once thought were extremely scarce turned out to be extremely common. Goods flooded onto eBay. More than half the traditional collecting categories experienced this phenomenon. Prices plummeted. Supply often exceeds demand.

The good news is that as eBay matures the secondary market in most categories has stabilized. Once again values can be tracked with confidence. The difficulty is getting old-time dealers and private collectors to accept this reality.

TIP In this instance, it is not about whether the object sells poorly or not but the fact that it sells.

You divided your objects into keep, sell, or toss piles. The objects in your sell piles represent money you do not have. Keeping or tossing them defeats the purpose. You win only when you sell.

When listing items for sale on eBay, start each item with a requested opening bid of $0.99. There will be objects that do not sell for anywhere near what you think they should have. Likewise there will be objects that sell for prices far in excess of what you expected. Honestly put, selling is a crapshoot. You roll the dice and take your chances.

FACT You cannot sell damaged items on eBay.

Objects sold on eBay have to be complete and in very good or better condition. They have to be room ready, that is, ready to use.

If an object shows signs of heavy use, is damaged in any way, visible on the surface or beneath, rusted, has parts missing, etc., put it in the junk pile. It "only has a little damage" does not play on eBay.

EBay buyers do not buy objects to restore. Further, do not get trapped in the logic that someone will buy an incomplete object to get the parts they need to complete an object they already own. Chances of this happening are slim to none.

● | FACT Antiques are a tough sell on eBay.

The average antiques and collectibles buyer on eBay is just over fifty years old. I was surprised when I learned this. I suspect you are too. The general assumption is that eBay buyers are younger buyers. This may be true for those buying new merchandise, but it is not for those buying antiques and collectibles.

Even given the fact that the average buyer is almost an antique himself, antiques at all levels on eBay.com struggle to achieve sale results that come close to matching auction and book prices. If an example does well, it is likely to be a high-end item.

● | FACT Statistics can be manipulated.

EBay statistics on the sale of antiques look far better than they are. LiveAuctions, a division of eBay providing Internet auction bidding services to auctioneers and auction houses, uses eBay as a platform. As a result eBay takes credit for the prices realized through LiveAuctions. While technically the object sold on eBay.com, the auctioneer or the auction house was the real seller.

Finally, a good general rule is the more common the object, the less likely it is to sell well on eBay. The number of potential buyers for any one item is finite, often no more than a few hundred. The number of identical objects often numbers in the thousands. Once all the buyers are satisfied, the secondary market collapses.

Alternatives to Selling It Yourself

If you would like to take advantage of the eBay marketplace, but do not want to do the selling yourself, there are alternatives.

FACT eBay is moving toward a one-stop shopping experience.

Consider hiring an eBay Trading Assistant. To obtain the location of one or more trading assistants in your area type "Trading Assistant" into the "Search" window on eBay's home page. A trading assistant, an experienced eBay seller, has to complete an eBay training program before being allowed to use this designation.

While some trading assistants will work from a client's home, most require the client to bring items for sale to them. Most work part-time, offering this service as a means of generating extra income. All are skilled in listing objects, answering customer service inquires, collecting payment, and concluding the sale.

Each trading assistant sets his own fees. Fees ranging from thirty-five to forty-five percent of the price realized plus reimbursement for all fees paid to eBay are the norm. Some trading assistants slide the percentage charged—the higher the price realized, the lower the fee.

TIP Insist on a contract or formal letter.

Home businesses often are very informal. Many do business on a handshake basis. You cannot afford to do this, especially if you are acting on behalf of an estate. Insist on a contract or a formal letter at the very least. The individual who tells you he would rather not put anything in writing is the same individual who is not reporting his income to the local, state, and federal government. You want nothing to do with these individuals.

In addition to eBay-trained sellers, many private individuals and some antiques malls also offer this service. Once again you need to check out qualifications and reputation of the individual or antiques mall before entrusting your objects to them.

Finally, franchise stores devoted to selling items on the Internet are slowly appearing across the United States. Check to see if one or more of them have locations in your area. The owners and employees are trained by the franchisee.

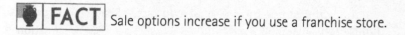 **FACT** Sale options increase if you use a franchise store.

Franchise stores take a broad approach to the Internet. They utilize a large variety of sale Web sites, not just eBay. They often have their own Web site store through which they sell direct.

Franchise Stores Focused on Selling on the Internet

Auction it TODAY, *www.auctionittoday.com*
Auction Depot, *www.eauction-depot.com*
iSold It, *www.i-soldit.com*
Quik Drop, *www.quikDrop.com*
Snappy Auctions, *www.snappyauctions.com*

Franchise stores also sell a much broader range of material than do eBay Trading Assistants, independent sellers, and antiques malls. A franchise store is capable of selling everything from a yacht to an egg beater.

Franchise store owners and employees have a solid knowledge of what they can and cannot sell successfully. They refuse more items than they accept. The one exception is when a new franchise opens and the store lacks merchandise.

Most franchise stores use a sliding percentage based on the price realized. The percentage can start as high as fifty percent. Once again the client is also expected to pay the fees charged by the Web site on which the item is sold.

Franchise stores often charge a listing fee if the object does not sell. Further, if the buyer insists on a reserve and the object does not sell, a buy-back fee is charged.

All franchise stores have formal contracts. Read any contract carefully before signing it.

Sale Options Exhausted

This exhausts your sale options. If you have not made your final decision of how to dispose of the objects you want to sell, this is the time to do it. If you have made your decision and sold your items, hopefully you did well.

You still have the items you planned to keep. Ideally all the items you wanted to sell did. Alas, it is far more likely that some did not. Now you have to get rid of those. The good news is there are only two choices remaining—donate or junk them.

CHAPTER TWELVE

Charitable Gifts

IT is necessary to start this chapter with three disclaimers. First, the Department of the Treasury's Internal Revenue Service's Charitable Contribution regulations constantly change, either through application or changes in the law. Second, I am not an accountant or attorney. Consult with one or both if you need the provisions of the law clarified or interpreted. Third, what follows applies only to federal tax deductions. Again consult with your accountant and/or attorney to determine what state laws may apply, if any.

If you are considering making a charitable donation of personal property, I recommend obtaining a copy of the Internal Revenue Service's Publication 526 entitled Charitable Contributions. While you can obtain a copy at any office of the Internal Revenue Service, it also is available on the Internet at *www.irs.gov/publication/p526.*

FACT This chapter applies only to the donation of personal property to charities. There are many other types of donations.

The IRS's Publication 526 is comprehensive. It covers donations of cash, stocks and bonds, personal property, vehicles, and much more. Although some information is general, the majority focuses solely on appreciating and depreciating personal property.

Is the Organization Entitled to Receive Deductible Contributions?

Tax exempt and tax deductible are not synonymous. Tax-exempt organizations do not have to pay income taxes. Although there are over twenty different categories of tax-exempt organizations, only a few of these can receive tax-deductible contributions.

If you are considering donating personal property, you want to seek an organization that has 501(c)(3), 501(c)(4), 501(c)(6), or 501(c)(19) status. When donating personal property, chances are you will be dealing with a 501(c)(3) organization.

TIP Keep your donations focused on organizations with 501(c)(3) status.

Most nonprofit organizations organized for charitable purposes are 501(c)(3) organizations. Purposes include charitable, educational, fostering national or international amateur sports competition, literary, prevention of cruelty to children or animals, religious, scientific, and testing for public safety.

The foundation status of a 501(c)(3) organization can limit the amount a person can donate. A public charity receives a substantial part of its income from the general public. The support can be direct or indirect. A private foundation receives most of its income from endowments and investments. Income is used to make grants to other organizations. A private foundation directs its earnings and assets to its parent organization. It does not make outside grants.

501(c)(4) organizations are focused on legislative lobbying; usually social welfare activities. Civic associations, employee associations, and some volunteer fire departments fall under these provisions. Deductions are taken as business expenses, not charitable contributions. As with most laws, there are exceptions where charitable contributions can be made, for example, war veterans' organizations where ninety percent of the members are veterans, and volunteer fire departments when the donation is used for public purposes.

501(c)(6) organizations include boards of trade, business leagues, chambers of commerce, real estate boards, and trade associations. Donations can be business deductions but not charitable donations.

501(c)(19) are veterans' organizations. Once again the ninety-percent rule applies before a gift can be a charitable deduction.

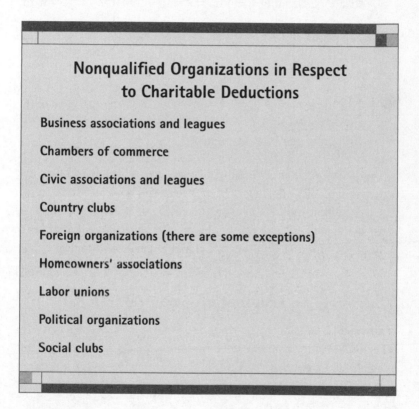

Nonqualified Organizations in Respect to Charitable Deductions

Business associations and leagues

Chambers of commerce

Civic associations and leagues

Country clubs

Foreign organizations (there are some exceptions)

Homeowners' associations

Labor unions

Political organizations

Social clubs

There are other organizations, such as cooperative hospital associations, which also can accept charitable donations. Most are cash and not personal property focused. However you most certainly will want to consider historical sites, museums, and other institutions that are managed by the United States, any state, the District of Columbia, a U.S. possession, state or U.S possession subdivisions, or an Indian tribal government. In order to be deductible, your contribution has to be used solely for public purposes.

TIP If an organization tells you they can accept charitable contributions and you are uncertain, consult your attorney, accountant, and/or the IRS.

Organizations must qualify to receive charitable gifts. If they meet federal guidelines but have not applied for qualification, your gifts will not be tax deductible.

FACT A qualified organization will be able to provide you with proof they are qualified.

Organizations that are qualified to receive charitable gifts have a letter from the IRS attesting to their status. You have a right to see it. The IRS's Publication 78, available at most public libraries, contains a list of organizations. Avoid problems. Do not make a donation to an organization that is not qualified and attempt to deduct it.

Valuing Personal Property Donations

The value of donated property given to a qualified organization is based on fair market value. Special rules apply to the donation of an airplane, boat, or car. When donating personal property to an organization, YOU are required to inform them that you are going to treat your gift as a charitable deduction.

FACT The Internal Revenue Service's publication 561 *Determining the Value of Donated Property* is a must-read.

You can obtain a copy of the IRS's Publication 561 at any Internal Revenue Service office or on the Internet at *www.irs.gov/publications/p561*. Non-cash gifts in excess of five hundred dollars are reported using Form 8283.

Fair market value has three critical components. It is the price at which the property would change hands between (1) a willing buyer and a willing seller, (2) neither having to buy or sell, and (3) both having reasonable knowledge of all the facts. Most individuals think of fair market value only in terms of the first two components. The third is equally important.

When downsizing or settling an estate, you are most likely to donate antiques, collectibles, and fine art objects, clothing, food, household goods, and jewelry and gems. Each has specific criteria that apply.

Antiques, Collectibles, and Fine Art Objects

Donations of antiques, collectibles, and fine art objects have to be supported by a written appraisal if the deduction to be claimed is over five thousand dollars. The IRS has established specific rules covering the information that is to be included in the appraisal and the qualifications of the appraiser.

FACT Objects of art, the IRS designation, is the same as fine art objects.

If the donation value of a single object exceeds fifty thousand dollars, a Statement of Value can be requested from the IRS. The IRS also has a series of rules that applies to the donation of collections. The same rules that apply to fine art objects are applied to collections.

Appraisal Fees

The fee you pay an appraiser to determine fair market value of a charitable donation does not qualify as a charitable donation. It may qualify as a personal expense if certain criteria are met. See IRS Publication 526.

Clothing, Used

Whether new or used, the fair market value for clothing is less than you paid for it. There is no fixed formula to determine this. Prices paid at consignment and thrift shops are often used to establish value.

Food

Special rules apply. The organization to which you are donating food should be able to assist you in what food qualifies and which does not. The three basic criteria are: (1) the food must be designated for the care of the ill, infants, or the needy, (2) the food must be used solely for the organization's charitable purpose, and (3) the organization does not sell or swap the food for other services. Obviously donated food also must meet federal guidelines for appearance, age, freshness, grade, etc.

Household Goods

Household goods, such as appliances, furniture, linens, etc., are another category where the fair market value is less than new. Replacement cost is not equivalent to fair market value. Although the IRS does not specifically suggest where to find values for these objects, values from garage sales, swap meets, and classified advertisements should provide sufficient guidelines.

Jewelry and Gems

This is a highly specialized area. Appraisals need to be done by a specialized jewelry appraiser. Ideally use an appraiser who also has completed his GIA training.

Keeping Proper Records

"Document, document, and document" is a good approach to take when gifting personal property to a charitable organization. Documents can include but are not limited to bills of sale, everything from clippings to auction catalogs documenting the sale of similar material, and the letter of gift from the charitable organization receiving the goods. You may not have to file all these documents with the IRS, but you should be prepared to make them available.

FACT Better too many records than too few.

General Considerations

Photograph every item that you donate. In the case of used clothing, food, and household goods, it is okay to group the material in lots. Just make certain that each piece is visible. Better too many photographs than too few.

If you have an appraisal done to determine the fair market value of your gift, restrictions often apply to the amount that you can actually deduct. Once again check with your accountant and/or attorney.

When donating any object, keep the following basic records—name and address of charity, date and time you made the donation and a reasonable description of what you donated, the fair market value with a brief explanation of how you arrived at it, your cost basis (if applicable), any terms or conditions placed on the gift, and a receipt or certificate of gift from the charitable organization acknowledging your gift.

Required Records

The reporting requirements for non-cash contributions, in this case personal property, depend on the value of the contribution. There are four break points: (1) less than $250; (2) $250 to $500; (3) $501 to $5,000; and, over $5,000. Each donation in the same calendar year does not stand alone. You need to total your donations to determine if you fall in the over-five-hundred-dollar categories.

TIP A conservative approach to valuing donated property is the best approach.

If your donation is less than $250, the only documentation needed is the name of the charitable organization, the date and location where the gift was made, and a reasonable description of the donated property. While not required to have a written receipt, you are advised to obtain one. A written letter from the charitable organization acknowledging the gift is acceptable.

When the gift falls in the $250 to $500 classification, a letter of gift from the charitable organization is required. The letter must include a description of the property donated, if you received any consideration as a result of the gift, and dated at or near the time of the donation. The letter does not have to include the fair market value of the donated property.

If your gift or gifts fall into the $500 to $5,000 classification, you now must indicate how you acquired the property, the approximate date, and the cost basis. If this information is not available, an explanation must be made.

An appraisal is required of donations totaling over $5,000 to a charitable organization. All the previous reporting requirements also apply.

FACT Do not allow all these rules to intimidate you.

Rules are intimidating. At this point, you are ready to sell or toss everything rather than go through the donation hassle.

There is no hassle if you keep good records and remain mindful of the rules. Chances are you are going to turn all the paperwork over to an accountant when tax preparation times rolls around. Your accountant will fill in the required blanks.

Charitable organizations need the public's support. Museums welcome the donation of objects that complement their mission statement and cost them nothing.

As stated earlier, the above information comes with two caveats. First, it applies to individual donations, not those from an estate. Second, it relates only to deductions made in conjunction with filing your federal taxes. Consult your attorney about the applicability of donations from an estate and your accountant on potential charitable deductions, if any, for state tax purposes.

What You Should Consider Donating

Why toss it if you can get a deduction? If the relatives do not want a family heirloom and the money it represents is not critical, consider donating it to a museum or historical society. Before you throw out perfectly good food, consider taking it to a food bank in your community.

TIP Be proactive when donating antiques, collectibles, and fine art objects.

Most individuals are aware of the donation value of antiques, collectibles, and fine art objects. The key is identifying the museum, historical society, or other institution, for example, a college or university, where the objects you plan to donate best belong. Visit prospective donor recipients. Talk with the museum's executive director, curator, or collections' manager. Ask point-blank about what role he sees for the objects you are offering. Check to make sure the organization has 501(c)(3) status. Finally, obtain a copy of their gift agreement and read it carefully.

TIP Ask specifically if the organization plans to add your gift to its collection or plans to sell it to raise funds to purchase objects it considers more appropriate to its collection.

Once you donate an object, ownership transfers to the organization. If your gift has conditions attached, the IRS will consider the extent of these restrictions when evaluating whether or not your gift qualifies as a true charitable contribution.

Likewise, if the organization does sell your gift within two years of the date of receipt, the organization must file Form 8282 with the Internal Revenue Service if the amount of your donated gift exceeded five hundred dollars. The IRS has the option of comparing the amount you claimed on Form 8283 against the amount on Form 8282. If there is a significant difference, chances are you will be hearing from the IRS. There are penalties for overstating the value of a donated gift. You can avoid this problem by inserting in the gift documentation a provision that the organization hold any objects you donate for two years and one day before selling them.

Donation Possibilities for Reusable Goods

APPLIANCES, MAJOR

Furniture bank
Goodwill Industries
Salvation Army
Thrift shop

BOOKS

**AAUW (local chapters often conduct
annual book sales)**
Library

CELL PHONES

See: *www.americancellphonedrive.org* or
www.charitablerecycling.com

CLOTHING AND ACCESSORIES

Disaster relief
Goodwill Industries
Homeless shelter
Salvation Army
Thrift shop

COMPUTERS

Furniture bank
Goodwill Industries

COSMETICS AND TOILETRIES

Salvation Army
Women's shelter

EYEGLASSES

Lions Club

FOOD

Disaster relief
Food bank
Homeless shelter

FURNITURE AND HOUSEHOLD GOODS

Churches (many churches hold annual rummage sales)
Furniture bank
Goodwill Industries
Salvation Army
Thrift shop

JEWELRY (REUSABLE)

Goodwill Industries
Thrift shop

PHONOGRAPH RECORDS

Library
College or university music department

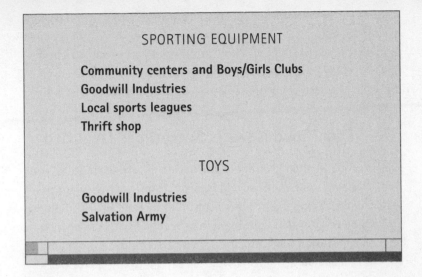

SPORTING EQUIPMENT

Community centers and Boys/Girls Clubs
Goodwill Industries
Local sports leagues
Thrift shop

TOYS

Goodwill Industries
Salvation Army

> 🏺 **TIP** Do not toss it if someone can use it.

While antiques, collectibles, and fine art objects are the first objects about which most individuals think in terms of donation, the simple truth is that anything that is in reusable condition is worth donating. Let your imagine run wild. Clothing, food, furniture, and household goods are the most obvious. Other possibilities include computers, game sets, televisions, office equipment, and toiletries. How about those hundreds of minibottles of mouthwash, shampoo, conditioner, bath gel, and hand lotion that you brought back from your travels? Battered women's shelters welcome these items.

> 🏺 **FACT** Do not transfer the task of junking your objects to a charitable organization.

Do not donate damaged or heavily worn goods. They are not reusable. They are junk. It is your responsibility to get rid of your junk, not the charitable organization's.

However beware of assuming that because you no longer have any use for an object, it is worthless to someone else. This is not the time to apply the criteria, "If I will not use it, what makes me think someone else will?" If an object is utilitarian and reusable, there is someone out there who would like to have it, especially if the cost is free.

Even Good News Is Sometimes Qualified

The amount of your charitable deduction is deducted from your total income. It is but one of many deductions, such as your mortgage interest. Taxes due are based on total income less deductions.

The end result is that your monetary benefit from a tax deduction depends on the tax bracket in which you find yourself. If you are in the twenty percent tax bracket, you are saving twenty percent of the total value of the donation in taxes.

Monetary benefit is not necessarily synonymous with personal benefit. The personal satisfaction that you did the right thing is more important.

FACT The value of your donation is not deducted from the taxes you owe.

The Final Step

You have kept it, sold it, or donated it. Hopefully, only a small amount remains. Only one small step remains before you can celebrate. You need to toss the rest.

But before you do, let's look over the remaining items. There may be hidden value in the junk. You have worked hard to get to this point. Invest a few more minutes or hours to ensure that you have maximized your potential income.

CHAPTER THIRTEEN

Junking It

CHANCES are you do not frequent scrap or salvage yards or landfill operations on a regular basis. Chances are you have NEVER been to a scrap yard or landfill in your entire life. Am I right?

Welcome to the possibility of an entirely new experience. It is not as bad or frightening as it may seem, especially if you keep in mind that you only need to do it once.

After deciding what you want to sell, keep, and donate, your toss piles should be small. The task is more a cleanup operation than a monumental challenge. On the other hand, some people actually have more junk than they do material worth selling, keeping, or donating.

TIP Do not cancel garbage service until the house is empty.

Ideally you have been bagging your junk as you sort through things and putting it out for pickup. Many garbage disposal services place a limit on the amount of garage they will collect during a pickup and have restrictions on the type of garbage that falls within their regular fee. Call the garbage disposal service and ask them to send you a copy of their pickup terms and conditions. Most garbage disposal services will take anything—the issue is how much extra do you have to pay them to do it.

Further the community, region, or state in which you are disposing of your junk may have recycling requirements. Make certain you know what they are and that you obey them. Be a good neighbor.

Who Is Going to Do the Cleanup?

Are you one of those individuals who does not like to get his hands dirty? Would you rather hire someone to this type of work than do it yourself? If yes, the answer is simple. Hire someone to do the work for you.

There are professionals who specialize in cleaning out homes. You can find them by checking the classified advertisements in a local newspaper or by checking a telephone directory; the newspaper is a likelier source.

The rates charged by a clean-out specialist vary. If you are asking them to dispose of junk, you will have to pay them a flat or per-hour fee. If they find enough salable and salvageable material to cover their time and produce a modest profit, they may offer to do the work for free. If there is a large quantity of salable and salvageable material, they actually may pay you a small amount.

♦ | TIP | The goal is to get the real estate broom clean.

Clean-out specialists leave a house broom clean. A broom-clean house is not ready for a white glove inspection. There still will be plenty of dirt and dust around. Consider hiring a cleaning service to make the place spic and span if you do not want to do this final cleanup chore.

If the cleanup challenge is minimal, there is no reason why you cannot do it yourself. If you are downsizing, you already have the supplies you need. If settling an estate, chances are it contains the necessary equipment and supplies. When the task is finished, junk the supplies and any cleaning equipment you do not want and take the balance with you.

The Final Profit Center

Not all junk is trash. Some of it may have salvage value. Visit one or more scrap yards in your area to check on the type of material they buy from private individuals. Chances are you will find a buyer for natural fiber textiles, base metals, and paper products. Not all gold, silver, and other precious metals have added collector, decorator, or reuse value. Often their only value is as melt. Look for buyers of this material as well.

Natural Fiber Textiles

Sell, keep, or donate all clothing and other textiles that are reusable. However, before junking the rest, divide it into two piles. Put clothing and other textiles made from animal and plant fibers, for example, cotton, linen, wool, etc., in the first pile. Clothing and textiles made from synthetic materials, such as polyester, go in the second pile. Take the first pile to the scrap yard. Toss the second pile.

Base Metals

Aluminum, brass, cast iron, copper, lead, tin, stainless steel, and zinc are the base metals you are most likely to encounter that have scrap value. Their value is maximized when they are sorted and sold by type.

If base metals are taken to a scrap yard and not separated, the scrap dealer buys them based on the scrap value of the least expensive metal in the pile. The price paid for objects such as appliances that contain a variety of material, some salvage and some not, is minimal.

There also are different grades of the same metal, with value differing by grade. Brass is divided into red, white, and yellow. Aluminum cans bring more per pound than does aluminum siding.

TIP | Many large appliances are still made primarily of metal.

You can take large appliances such as washers, dryers, and refrigerators to a scrap yard. You will not receive much, perhaps only a few dollars. However, if taken as part of a larger lot, every little bit adds up.

Appliances that contain Freon, for example, old air conditioners, freezers, and refrigerators, must have the Freon removed before a scrap yard will accept them. Check the phone book for companies that specialize in Freon removal. When the Freon is removed, the removal company will tag the appliance. Also, doors on freezers and refrigerators must be removed prior to taking them to a scrap yard or placing them out on a curb for pickup.

There is more metal in a house than most people realize. Tools often contain large amounts of metal. Pots and pans are made from aluminum, cast iron, and stainless steel. Some have copper bottoms, which must be cut off to maximize the return. Old motors have cast metal housings and copper-wound rotors.

For additional information about salvageable metals, revisit or read "Scrap" in the "To Toss or Not to Toss?" section of chapter four.

Paper Products

Divide paper up into newsprint, glossy paper, and cardboard. Newsprint is paper made out of wood pulp, like newspaper. It can also include bulk mail, correspondence, printouts, etc. Start filling boxes with recyclable paper as you sort. Recyclable paper is purchased by weight. The scrap dealer does not care what form it is in.

FACT Destroy personal records. Do not scrap them.

The world does not need to know your business or that of the deceased. Destroy all personal records. In fact, if local ordinances allow burning, burn them. Purchasing a shredding machine is an alternative. However, if you plan to sell the shredded paper for scrap, make certain it is thoroughly mixed so that the possibilities of piecing it back together are improbable.

Some recycling centers now offer free shredding service while you watch. A number even advertise this fact on television. Touted as free for private individuals, businesses may have to pay a fee.

Glossy paper is a tough sell. Some salvage yards take it, others do not. Check first before taking it. Most magazines, mail-order catalogs, and some bulk mail pieces are printed on glossy paper. Many newspaper inserts are printed on glossy stock. Separate these from the newsprint. If you do not, the scrap dealer will lower the price he is willing to pay.

TIP You do not want to take anything to a scrap yard that you may have to haul back.

Cut up corrugated cardboard and tie it in bundles. Do not mix pasteboard, the material from which most household boxes, for example, cereal, clothing, and shoe boxes are made with the corrugated cardboard. Some scrap yards will only accept corrugated cardboard for recycling and not pasteboard. Once again, check before assuming they will.

■ | FACT | Books are made of paper.

The vast majority of books are tough to resell. The AAUW, local libraries, and other organizations that conduct annual book sales are getting fussier and fussier about the type of books they accept as donations. Hundreds of nonsalable books are not something with which you will want to deal either. No problem! Books are made of paper. Box them and take them to a scrap dealer.

Precious Metals

Everyone likes to think that the precious metal objects they own, whether a flatware service or jewelry, has more collecting value than scrap value. Alas this often is not the case. The pair of concrete-weighted 1920s/1930s sterling silver candlesticks that belonged to your grandparents sparks little interest in the collecting, decorating, and reuse community. They are purchased primarily for melt. The metal will be recycled to make a new product.

Gold

For centuries gold has been melted down, re-refined, and recycled. Further recycled gold, also known as scrap gold, plays an important role in the gold market. When times are tough or gold prices rise, the gold scrap supply increases dramatically.

■ | FACT | Old and unwanted gold can bring good scrap prices.

Gold is graded by karat, with 24-karat being pure gold. Pure gold is soft. Other materials have to be added to gold to harden it. Hence

12-karat gold consists of half its weight in gold and half in other material.

Scrap gold exists in a wide variety of forms, including coins, eyeglass frames, dental fillings, jewelry, pocket and wristwatch housings, etc. Dental crowns, bridges, fillings, and teeth are usually made from 16-karat gold. Jewelry includes bracelets, chains, earrings, and rings.

FACT Not all gold is marked.

While the English, French, and some other European countries' hallmark systems predate the eighteenth century, manufacturers in other countries, including the United States, did not start marking gold until the late nineteenth century. Gold should be tested to determine its karat.

Many individuals often think gold-plated items are karat gold. If just the surface is tested, the results will be positive. The surface plating is karat gold. Make certain the test area extends well below the surface.

FACT Plated gold items have no melt value.

In the 1950s many ceramic manufacturers of dinnerware and tabletop accessories heavily gilded their pieces and marked them 22K or 24K. Unfortunately unknowledgeable individuals see these pieces and assume they are rich. However the amount of gold on these items is measured in pennies if not a percent of a penny. The cost to recover the gold is far more than the process is worth.

Most jewelers will buy scrap gold and other precious metals and advertise this fact in newspaper display advertisements and in telephone directories. Before approaching them, check on the current scrap value of gold.

● | FACT The value of scrap precious metals changes on a day-to-day basis.

Dealers buying precious metals for melt work on a fifteen- to twenty-percent margin. They turn around their purchases instantly. They also pay less as the karat percentage decreases. Most buyers post the prices they pay. If you have a large quantity of gold to sell, you should expect to receive a slightly higher price.

● | FACT Always check the value of the object on the collector, decorator, and reuse markets before selling it for scrap.

Gold jewelry, especially if dating prior to 1915, is usually worth far more on the collector market than on the scrap market. This also applies to gold coins with a condition grade of 50 plus. If a piece has high aesthetic qualities and/or its manufacture based on the work of an internationally recognized designer, it should not be sold for scrap. If you have the slightest doubt, check.

Silver

The American and British standard is sterling, 925 parts silver per thousand. Once again, while the English use of the sterling standard predates the eighteenth century, American manufacturers did not adopt it universally until the end of the nineteenth century. Other countries used different standards, for example, Germany uses 800 parts silver per thousand. You will encounter foreign pieces with numbers as low as 800 and as high as 950.

The amount of silver in coin silver varies. Ideally it should be around 900 parts per thousand. However it can be as low as 750 parts per thousand.

There is no silver in German silver and nickel silver. The terms describe the surface color; German silver is not silver from Germany. However, pieces marked Mexican silver should be tested. They often have a high silver content.

> ● | FACT | Most pocket silver, that is, circulated silver coins from someone's pocket, only has melt value.

Pocket silver, preclad dollars, half dollars, quarters, and dimes, is the most commonly found form of melt silver. Coins are graded on a scale of 1 to 75, with 75 being the highest grade. Collectors focus on coins graded 50 or higher, with 60 to 65 being the minimum grade for an "investment" coin.

When buying pocket silver, dealers pay so much times face value rather than taking the time to grade each coin individually. Face value means the actual value of the coin, for example, a fifty-cent piece, times a fixed price. In the last twenty years the face price for pocket silver has been as low as four dollars to as high as fifty dollars.

Once again check the collector, decorator, and reuse markets before selling any silver for melt.

Platinum

When most people are asked to name the most expensive common precious metal, they answer gold. Wrong! Platinum is the answer. The value of platinum is not quite double the value of gold.

> ● | TIP | Do not let someone try to tell you that the platinum ring setting you are trying to sell is silver or white gold.

Tests exist for platinum, just as they do for gold and silver. When a jeweler or other individual is testing your metal, insist on being present. If you do not understand what is happening, ask to have the process explained to you.

Junking It

At long last you are left with the junk. The only choice remaining is the landfill. Sad but true, the best home for some objects is the dump.

Dumpster

If the amount of material you are planning to junk is overwhelming, rent a Dumpster. Dumpsters for household use come in sizes ranging from ten yards to forty yards.

You pay a set price to rent a Dumpster. The first ton of garbage is included in the price. Hopefully you will not even come close to reaching this poundage. However, if you do exceed it, expect to pay an additional per-ton fee.

Dumpsters generally rent by the week, so do not rent a Dumpster until you need it.

FACT There are things you cannot throw into a Dumpster.

The United States Resource Conservation & Recovery Act of 1976 defines items that are considered hazardous waste. You cannot dispose of these items in a landfill. You must make special arrangements. Do not attempt to get around the law by burying the items deep in legitimate disposal goods.

Landfill

If you do not wish to rent a Dumpster and you have more to junk than your regular garbage disposal service will pick up, you need to get what remains to your local landfill. Put the material in your passenger vehicle or pickup truck if you are lucky to own one or have a friend who will loan you his. If not, you will have to rent a van.

Hazardous Waste

CHARACTERISTICS

Corrosive, for example, acids and bases
Ignitable, for example, oils, organic liquids, and solvents
Reactive, for example, alkali metals and oxidizing agents
Toxic, for example, heavy metals and organometallic
    compounds
Unstable, for example, perchlorates and peroxides

SOME EXAMPLES

Batteries containing lead, mercury, or other heavy metals
Bulbs and lamps containing mercury vapor
"E-Waste," for example, computers, electronic equipment,
    cell phones, and lasers
Tiles, old flooring or roofing, containing asbestos
"Sharps," for example, needles, syringes

TIP If you sit in your car when it is weighed the first time, make certain you sit in it when it is weighed the second time.

When you arrive at the landfill, your vehicle will be weighed. You next will drive to a series of Dumpsters and unload your junk. When finished your vehicle will be weighed a second time. The price you pay is based on the weight of the material you are placing in the landfill.

Most landfills will allow you to dump large appliances and other recyclable material at their recycling area at no charge. Call in advance to see if such a service is provided and what type of material qualifies. Also do not forget to ask if they provide shredding services for personal papers.

If you have rented a large van, for example, a cube van, step van, etc., you must drive up into the landfill and deposit your junk in a designated area. When doing this, you are required to wear an orange vest and hard hat. Do not expect the landfill to provide them. You need to take them with you.

Done at Last

You are done. CELEBRATE. You have sold, kept, or tossed it. Your job is done.

If this is the case, why is there one more chapter in this book? The answer is simple. The process could have been simplified and far less work, if the individual who owned all this material had taken a few initiatives during his or her lifetime.

This also applies to you. You and your heirs will eventually face the same needs and concerns that you have just faced. For this reason and this reason alone, do not close this book now. Keep reading.

CHAPTER FOURTEEN

WARM HAND VERSUS COLD HAND: What Is Going to Happen to All My Stuff When I Die?

CHANCES are you love the things you own. They are the memories of a lifetime. Disposing of them would be painful. Yet as one gets older the pressure builds.

"There is nothing here that I want. Get rid of your things now so I am not faced with the problem," kids implore.

"What's going to happen to all your stuff when you die?" friends ask.

Alas, "to hell with you" and "none of your business" are not valid answers in the real world (although there is no penalty for thinking that!).

> 🏺 **FACT** There is absolutely no reason why this has to be your problem.

If you think about these two questions carefully, there is a simple truth that applies. When you die, disposing of your things is not your problem. If you cannot bear to part with any-thing, then do not do it. Your things are who you are. It is per-fectly acceptable to die with them. Let your heirs earn their inheritance the old-fashioned way—with hard work to maximize their return.

On the other hand, a little preplanning will make the executor(s)' task easier. Additionally, disposing of unwanted goods during your lifetime puts the money in your pocket. Feel free to spend it—travel, buy something you always wanted but could never afford, enjoy life. Give meaning to the bumper stickers and T-shirts that read: "I am spending my child's inheritance."

Consult an attorney and draw up a will. The following advice deals only with personal property. The terms of your will should express your wishes for everything that encompasses your estate.

Your Wishes

If you want a specific piece of personal property to go to a specific person or institution, state this clearly in your will. If you have not asked the person or institution if they will accept the property, con-sider the possibility that they may refuse. Provide a second option.

If your list is extensive, you may want to attach it to the will. In order to make the list binding, clearly state in the will that the list constitutes your express wishes. If you draw up the list yourself, attach it to the will with a paper clip or staple, and do not note its existence in the will, your executor is not necessarily legally bound to honor it. Your list now has become a suggestion rather than mandatory.

Some people mark and tag pieces with the name of the individ-ual to whom they promised or hoped to give the pieces once they pass away. In many cases this is done on a walk-through with chil-dren and grandchildren. An executor is not legally bound to honor these wishes, even if the handwriting is in the hand of the owner.

📍 TIP Beware of the question "Can I have that when you die?"

People do not like to say no. As a person gets older, family and friends often express an interest in specific objects. Rather than say no, the older person merely smiles or answers evasively. The person asking always interprets this as a yes.

The ideal situation is to promise nothing. This will not happen. Promises will be made. Alas, they also will be forgotten. Few individuals write them down. The end result is confusion and occasionally great difficulty following the death of the individual.

📍 TIP Before agreeing to will or pass along an object, check first to see that your wishes will be honored.

When you will an object to someone, the implication is that the recipient will treasure and cherish the object just as you did. This is not always the case. The two key questions are: (1) Does the person or institution really want it?, and (2) Will the person or institution care for the object with the same passion as I do? Do not be afraid to ask the recipient these questions. Especially in the case of items of great value, if it is important to you that they stay in the family, check that the family member who is asking for them is not planning on selling them.

Who Gets It?

You are not Solomon. However you do own your possessions. You, and you alone, make the final decision about who gets what. Not everyone will accept this. Immediate family, especially children and siblings, feel they have the right to tell you what to do. No, they do not. The things you own are your things. You get to decide.

There is no law that says you have to treat everyone equally. You have every right to reward those you like and ignore those you do not. The pressure will be intense to conform to an "equal division" doctrine. Everyone wants what they believe to be their fair share. Once again this is for you, not them to determine. Although, if it is important to you that your children maintain close relationships among themselves once you are gone, it might be wise to try to avoid creating resentment among them.

There is no right or wrong priority order. Nowhere does it say children have to come first. You establish the order.

Family Treasures

The value of family treasures is sentimental and emotional. While the value also can be monetary, this does not necessarily have to be the case.

FACT The value is in the story.

It is the stories associated with family objects that make them valuable. If this is to continue, you need to pass down the story with the object. Write it down. Do not trust oral transmission. Oral stories get distorted and embellished as they pass from one generation to another.

Many family objects are associated with specific individuals. Their story needs to be passed down as well. A photograph of the individual accompanying the object further enhances its meaning to the next generation.

Pass down your family treasures in as good or better condition than you inherited them. If you have the funds and a piece needs restoration, have it done. Take older framed objects to a custom framing shop and have the matting and backing brought up to modern standards.

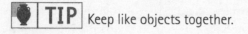 **TIP** Keep like objects together.

If you have a pair of something, do not divide them between two individuals. These objects have pair or set value, that is, their value is increased when they are together. The same holds true for dinnerware, flatware, and stemware services. If you have a large—that is, twelve place settings or more—dinnerware or flatware service, you might consider dividing it half. However a problem arises when you get to the service pieces unless you are willing to go on the secondary market and buy the required duplicates.

A Case Study

In Pennsylvania German country, dinnerware, flatware, and stemware services are usually divided by form. For example, in a flatware service, one person gets the spoons, another the knives, another the forks, etc.

Uncle Bob was the family spoon man. When he died, Uncle Bob had over two hundred spoons from a variety of different flatware services in a buffet drawer. He had no knives, forks, or serving pieces to match.

When it comes to family tradition, asking the "why" question is not always a good idea.

Identify the relatives. The problem with family photographs is that the person who received them knew the people in them. When that person dies, the information is lost. Historical societies have album after album, box after box of family pictures with no idea whatsoever who the individuals are. These images are affectionately known in the trade as "instant relatives." If you do not label your family photographs, chances are the next generation is simply going to throw them out. One good idea for labeling family photos is to make color copies of the photos and write the names of the family members on the color copy, then clip it to the back of the frame of the photo.

TIP As hard as it is to do, you need to ask yourself, "Is the family the best place for the family treasures?"

Your heirs may not be the best recipient for your family treasures. If they do not care, chances are that within a short time of receiving them, they will sell them. This may not be what you want.

You need to look honestly at the financial capabilities, lifestyle, and environment of any possible heir. A child or grandchild who has problems managing money or has a tendency toward alcoholism or drugs may not be a wise choice.

You have plenty of choices besides family. A local, regional, state, or federal managed historic site, historical society, or museum is one alternative. Again, check first with family to determine if any interest exists. If not, or if the interested party is unacceptable, check the interest level of any institution or organization to which you plan to gift your family treasures.

Collection

Collectors collect in a vacuum. They are loath to share information, especially what they paid, with a spouse, family, or friends. This is a mistake, albeit one made frequently. If you are a collector, you should take at least one person into your confidence and, at the very minimum, share where the purchase records and other information relating to value are located. Easily stated, few do it.

Most collections are not inventoried. Collectors would rather devote their time acquiring and playing with their collections than on the tedious task of record posting. However, there are many easy-to-use computer database programs that make this task much simpler. Digitally photographing pieces and writing a brief caption that includes an estimated value is a good start.

I must admit, this is definitely a "do as I say, not as I do" situation in terms of my own collections. Who has time to catalog items when there are books and columns to write, personal appearances to attend, television shows to tape, and radio broadcasts to do. You may feel the same way, and not have the time to properly inventory your collection.

If nothing else, create a suggested disposal plan and attach it to the will. The plan should include a list of individuals, for example, auctioneers, collectors, and dealers, who the collector feels the family can trust to provide them with good advice.

FACT What looks like total chaos to the uninitiated may be order to the collector.

Collectors tend to display and store related objects within close proximity to one another. If a collector has multiple collections, these divisions are often quite obvious. If a single collection, they may not be. In the collector's mind, a single collection often is divided into a dozen or more subcategories. As a collector, you need to make your executor aware of what these subcategories are and how best to dispose of them.

Disposing of a collection or collections is often more painful and gut-wrenching than disposing of family heirlooms. You do not have to do this if you do not want to do it. However, there is one truth you do need to face—you and you alone are in the best position to see that the disposal is done correctly.

Dying with your collection or collections intact is perfectly acceptable. However, once again, the money represented might be put to better use in the final years of your life.

Odds and Ends

Chances are your home is filled more with odds and ends—that is, the objects used as part of everyday life—than family treasures and collections. As one gets older, one develops a realization that one tends to own far more than is required to live comfortably.

When you reach the point when you recognize this, start liquidating the things you no longer need. Give them away. Donate to a church bazaar or other charitable organization. Sell them at a garage sale.

TIP Establish a time period, usually one to two years, to determine how important a utilitarian object is to you. If you have not used it during this time period, question its importance.

When you are done, do not be surprised if you do not miss any of this material. Chances are you did not use it very often or at all. Delight in the fact that the objects are now someone else's disposal problem, and you have some found money in your pocket.

The Warm Hand

Disposing of your things prior to death is known as dealing with the issue with a warm hand rather than a cold one. It sounds gruesome, and it is, but it makes the point.

There is satisfaction in knowing that the things you treasure will be loved and cherished by the next generation as well. Giving with a warm hand also allows you to tell the stories that accompany your treasures. Consider videotaping yourself with your children or grandchildren as you tell them the family stories that each item brings to mind. The treasures will be that much more meaningful when the family has heard the stories from you, and can pass the stories on. The warm hand disposal method is not for everyone, but everyone should consider it. You may find that it brings you great joy to see your children and grandchildren wearing your heirloom jewelry and using your good silver on holidays.

When It Is Gone, It Is Gone

Once you give or donate an object, it is gone. You no longer own it nor do you have any ownership rights in it unless your gift included such restrictions. The new owner is free to do whatever they wish with your gift.

Promises made orally are often ignored. The person or institution who received your gift may experience a change in circumstances that may make honoring promises difficult or impossible. Even a promise in writing is no guarantee that it will be honored long-term.

FACT Out of sight, out of mind.

Most people, especially if they are collectors, have trouble letting go. They find it hard to resist the temptation to visit their former possession. What happens is that they do not see the object, but the situation in which it is being displayed or used. They cannot resist the urge to nitpick. Past memories and dreams cloud the present reality.

When visiting family, resist the urge to ask to see your former possessions or to criticize how they are being used. Do not create a difficult situation that taints the generosity of your gift.

Once an object is given away, walk away. You made a conscious decision to end your association with it. Trust and accept the fact that you made the right decision.

One Last Thought

A sign in the office of the president of the board of directors of the Historical Society of York County (Pennsylvania) when I was executive director, read "No Decision Is a Decision." I remember the sign quite distinctly because the person in whose office it hung was famous for this very tactic.

You do not have to make a decision about disposing of your things, either with a warm hand or cold one. It is okay.

If you do not decide, the government will. Inheritance laws are very detailed. The settlement and division may not be according to your wishes, but you will not know.

The right answer rests with you. Hopefully *Sell, Keep, or Toss?* has made your final (a pun definitely intended) decision or decisions easier.

Appendix I

Auction Houses

American auction houses divide into three groups—national, regional, and specialized. Supplementing this list are thousands of local auctioneers who sell in rented halls and off back porches across America.

When you're searching for an auction house, the websites *www.auctioneers.org*, *www.auctionzip.com*, and *www.kansasauctioneers.com* (links to those states that have auctioneers associations) are good places to start. Also check out these auction houses and auctioneers.

Alderfer Auction Company
501 Fairgrounds Rd.
Hatfield, PA 19440
215-393-3000
www.alderferauction.com
Regional

Arthur Auctioneering
563 Reed Road
Hughesville, PA 17737
800-278-4873
www.auctionzip.com/PA-Auctioneers
Specialty: Stoneware

Auction Team Köln
Postfach 50 11 1
D-50971 Köln
Germany
Jane Herz, USA Representative
941-925-0385
www.breker.com
Specialty: Historic Business Equipment, Scientific Instruments

Noel Barrett Antiques & Auctions Ltd.
PO Box 300
Carversville, PA 18913
215-297-5109
www.noelbarrett.com
Specialty: Toys

Bonhams
595 Madison Avenue, 6th Floor
New York, NY 10022
212-644-9001
www.bonhams.com/us
National/International

Bonhams & Butterfield
220 San Bruno Avenue
San Francisco, CA 94103
415-861-7500
www.bonhams.com/us
National/International

Cerebo
PO Box 327
East Prospect, PA 17317
800-695-2235
www.cerebro.com
Specialty: Cigar Memorabilia

Cohasco, Inc
PO Box 821
Yonkers, NY 10702
914-476-8500
Regional

Cowan's Historic Americana Auctions
673 Wilmer Avenue
Cincinnati, OH 45226
513-871-1670
www.historicamericana.com
Specialty: Americana

Craftsman Auctions
333 North Main Street
Lambertville, NJ 08530
609-397-9374
www.ragoarts.com
Specialty: Art Nouveau,
Arts and Crafts, and Art Deco

Dawson & Nye
128 The American Road
Morris Plains,NJ 07950
973-984-6900
www.dawsonandnye.com
Regional

Doyle New York
175 E. 87th St.
New York, NY 10128
212-427-2730
www.doylenewyork.com
Regional

Flomaton Antique Auction
PO Box 1017
Flomaton, AL 36441
251-296-3059
www.flomatonantiqueauction.com
Regional

Garth's Auctions
2690 Stratford Road
PO Box 369
Delaware, OH 43015
740-362-4771
www.garths.com
Regional and Specialist
in Country and Folk Art

Glass Works Auctions
PO Box 180
East Greenville, PA 18041
215-679-5849
www.glswrk-auction.com
Specialty: Bottles and Shaving Memorabilia

Hake's Americana & Collectibles
1966 Greenspring Drive
Timonium, MD 21093
410-427-9440
www.hakes.com
Specialty: Twentieth Century Collectibles

Tom Harris Auctions
203 S. 18th Avenue
Marshalltown, IA 50158
641-754-4890
www.tomharrisauctions.com
Regional

Norman C. Heckler & Company
79 Bradford Corner Road
Woodstock Valley, CT 06282
860-974-1634
www.hecklerauction.com
Regional

Heritage Auction Galleries
3500 Maple Avenue, 17th Floor
Dallas, TX 75219
800-872-6467
www.americana.heritageauctions.com
*Specialties: Coins, Twentieth
Century Collectibles, Stamps*

Leslie Hindman Auctioneers
122 North Aberdeen Street
Chicago, IL 60607
312-280-1212
www.lesliehindman.com
National/Regional

Jackson's Auctioneer's & Appraisers
2229 Lincoln Street
Cedar Falls, IA 50613
319-277-2256
www.jacksonsauction.com
Regional

James D. Julia, Inc.
203 Showhegan Road
PO Box 830
Fairfield, ME 04937
207-453-7125
www.juliaauctions.com
Regional

Kruse International
5540 County Road 11A
Auburn, IN 46706
800-968-4444
www.kruse.com
Specialty: Cars

Lang's Sporting Collectables, Inc.
663 Pleasant Valley Road
Waterville, NY 13480
(315) 841-4623
www.langsauctions.com
Specialty: Hunting and Fishing

Majolica Auctions
200 North Main
PO Box 332
Wolcottville, IN 46795
260-854-2859
www.strawserauctions.com
Specialty: Majolica

Mastro Auctions
115 W. 22nd Street, Ste. 125
Oak Brook, IL 60523
630-472-1200
www.mastroauctions.com
*Specialty: Sports Collectibles,
Twentieth Century Collectibles*

Wm. Morford
R. D. #2, Cobb Hill Road
Cazenovia, NY 13035
315-662-7625
www.morfauctions.com
Regional

Norton Auctioneers
50 W. Pearl Street
Coldwater, MI 49036
517-279-9063
www.nortonauctioneers.com
Regional

Richard Opfer
1919 Greenspring Drive
Timonium, MD 21093
410-252-5035
www.opferauction.com
Regional

Pettigrew Auction Co.
1645 South Tejon Street
Colorado Springs, CO 80906
719-633-7963

Pook & Pook, Inc.
463 East Lancaster Avenue
PO Box 268
Downingtown, PA 19335
610-269-4040
www.pookandpook.com
Regional

Rago Modern Auctions
333 North Main Street
Lambertville, NJ 08530
609-397-9374
www.ragoarts.com
Specialty: Art Nouveau, Arts and
Crafts, Art Deco, Modernism

Red Baron's Antiques
6450 Roswell Road
Atlanta, GA 30328
404-252-3770
www.redbaronsantiques.com
Regional

L. H. Selman Ltd.
123 Locust Street
Santa Cruz, CA 95060
800-538-0766
www.paperweight.com
Specialty: Paperweights

Skinner, Inc
Bolton Gallery
357 Main Street
Bolton, MA 01740
978-779-6241
www.skinnerinc.com
National/Regional

Skinner, Inc.
Boston Gallery
The Heritage On The Garden
63 Park Plaza
Boston, MA 02116
617-350-5400
www.skinnerinc.com
National/Regional

Sloans & Kenyon
7034 Wisconsin Avenue
Chevy Chase, MD 20815
301-634-2330
www.sloansandkenyon.com
Regional

Smith & Jones, Inc., Auctions
12 Clark Lane
Sudbury, MA 01776
978-443-5517
www.smithandjonesauctions.com
Specialty: Stoneware

R. M. Smythe & Co., Inc.
2 Rector Street, 12th Floor
New York, NY 10006
800-662-1880
www.smytheonline.com
Specialty: Paper Ephemera

SoldUSA, Inc.
1418 Industrial Drive, Box 11
Matthews, NC 28105
704-815-1500
www.soldusa.com
Specialty: Hunting and Fishing

Sotheby's New York
1334 York Avenue
New York, NY 10021
541-312-5683
www.sothebys.com
National/International

Swann Galleries, Inc.
104 E. 25th Street
New York, NY 10010
212-254-4710
www.swanngalleries.com
Specialty: Books, Prints, Paper Ephemera

The Three Rivers
PO Box 6298
Pittsburgh, PA 16212
724-222-3332
www.3riversauction.com
Regional

Tool Shop Auctions
Tony Murland
78 High Street
Needham Market
Suffolk, 1P6 8AW
England
+44 (0)1449 722992
www.antiquetools.co.uk
Specialty: Tools

John Toomey Gallery
818 North Boulevard
Oak Park, IL 60301
708-383-5234
www.treadwaygallery.com
*Specialty: Art Nouveau, Arts and Crafts,
Art Deco, Modernism*

Treadway Gallery, Inc.
2029 Madison Road
Cincinnati, OH 45208
513-321-6742
www.treadwaygallery.com
*Specialty: Art Nouveau, Arts and Crafts,
Art Deco, Modernism*

Weschler's
909 E. Street, NW
Washington, D.C. 20004
202-628-1281
www.wechlers.com
Regional

York Town Auction Inc.
815 North George Street
York, PA 17404
717-848-8400
www.yorktownauction.net
Regional

Appendix II

Antiques & Collectibles Trade Newspapers

NATIONAL MAGAZINES

Antiques & Collecting Magazine
1006 S. Michigan Avenue
Chicago, IL 60605
800-762-7576
www.acmagazine.com
e-mail: greg@acmagazine.com

Collectors News
506 Second Street
PO Box 306
Grundy Center, IA 50638
800-352-8039
www.collectors-news.com
e-mail:collectors@collectors-news.com

The Magazine Antiques
575 Broadway
New York, NY 10012
800-925-8059
e-mail: brantpubs@aol.com

NATIONAL NEWSPAPERS

The Antique Trader Weekly
Krause Publications
700 East State Street
Iola, WI 549 45
800-726-9966 or 888-457-2873
www.antiquetrader.com
e-mail: antiquetrader@krause.com

Antiques and the Arts Weekly
The Bee Publishing Co.
PO Box 5503
Newtown, CT 06470
203-426-3141
www.antiquesandthearts.com
e-mail: antiques@thebee.com

AntiqueWeek (Central and Eastern Editions)
27 Jefferson Street
PO Box 90
Knightstown, IN 46148
800-876-5133
www.antiqueweek.com
e-mail: subscriptions@antiqueweek.com

Auction Action Antique News
1404 E. Green Bay Street
Shawano, WI 54166
715-524-3076
www.auctionactionnews.com
e-mail: auctionactionnews.com

Maine Antique Digest
911 Main Street
PO Box 1429
Waldoboro, ME 04572
800-752-8521
www.maineantiquedigest.com
e-mail: mad@maine.com

REGIONAL NEWSPAPERS AND MAGAZINES

NEW ENGLAND

Antique Review East
Insert in The Antique Trader Weekly
antiquereview@krause.com

The Journal of Antiques and Collectibles
PO Box 950
Sturbridge, MA 01566
888-698-0734
e-mail: tothejournal@aol.com

New England Antiques Journal
24 Water Street
Palmer, MA 01069
800-432-3505
www.antiquesjournal.com
e-mail: visit@antiquejournal.com

Northeast Journal of Antiques & Arts
24 Water Street
Palmer, MA 01069
800-432-3505
www.antiquesjournal.com

UnRavel the Gavel
PO Box 983
Laconia, NH 03247
603-524-4281
www.thegavel.net
e-mail: gavel96@worldpath.net

MIDDLE ATLANTIC STATES

Antique Review East
Insert in The Antique Trader Weekly
antiquereview@krause.com

Antiques & Auction News
PO Box 500
Mount Joy, PA 17552
800-800-1833
www.antiquesandauctionnews.net
e-mail: antiquesnews@engleonline.com

Renninger's Antique Guide
2 Cypress Place
PO Box 495
Lafayette Hill, PA 19444
877-385-0104
www.renningers.com

SOUTH

The Antique Gazette
PO Box 1529
Deham Springs, LA 70727
225-665-1611
www.theantiquesgazette.com

The Antique Shoppe
PO Box 2175
Keystone Heights, FL 32656
352-475-1679
www.antiqueshoppefl.com
e-mail: antshoppe@aol.com

Cotton & Quail Antique Gazette
700 East State
Iola, WI 54992
888-457-2873
www.antiquetrader.com

Southeastern Antiquing & Collecting
Magazine
PO Box 510
Acworth, GA 30101
888-388-7827
www.gostar.com
e-mail: antiquing@go-star.com

Southern Antiques
PO Drawer 1107
Decatur, GA 30031
888-800-4997
e-mail: southernantiques@mns.com

MIDWEST

The Antique Collector and Auction Guide
c/o Farm and Dairy
185-205 East State Street
PO Box 38
Salem, OH 44460
330-337-3419
www.farmanddairy.com

Antique Review Midwest
Insert in The Antique Trader
e-mail: antiquereview@krause.com

Collectors Journal
1800 West D Street
PO Box 601
Vinton, IA 52349
319-472-4763
www.collectorsjournal.com
e-mail: connie@collectorsjournal.com

Discover Mid-America
104 East 5th Street, Ste. 201
Kansas City, MO 64106
800-899-9730
www.discoverypub.com
e-mail: publisher@discoverypub.com

Great Lakes Trader
131 S. Putnam
Williamstown, MI 48895
800-785-6367
e-mail: gltrader@aol.com

The Old Times Newspaper
PO Box 340
Maple Lake, MN 55358
800-539-1810
www.theoldtimes.com
e-mail: oldtimes@theoldtimes.com

Yesteryear
PO Box 2
Princeton, WI 54968
www.yesteryearpublications.com
e-mail: yesteryear@vbe.com

SOUTHWEST

The Antique Register
PO Box 84345
Phoenix, AZ 85071
602-942-8950
www.countryregister.com
e-mail: info@countryregister.com

Parker's Antique News
PO Box 656
Mineola, TX 75773
800-446-3588
e-mail: antq@dctexas.net

MOUNTAIN STATES

Mountain States Collector
PO Box 2525
Evergreen, CO 80437
303-674-1253
www.mountainstatescollector.com
e-mail: spreepub@mac.com

WEST COAST

Antique & Collectables Monthly News
Magazine
500 Fesler, Ste. 201
PO Box 12589
El Cajon, CA 92022
619-593-2925
e-mail:ac@krause.com

Antique Journal
500 Fesler, Ste. 201
PO Box 12589
El Cajon, CA 92022
e-mail: antiquejournal@krause.com

Old Stuff
VBM Printers, Inc.
PO Box 449
McMinnville, OR 97128
503-434-5386
www.oldstuffnews.com
e-mail: oldstuff@oldstuffnews.com

West Coast Peddler
PO Box 5134
Whittier, CA 90607
562-698-1718
www.westcoastpeddler.com
e-mail: westcoastpeddler@earthlink.net

INTERNATIONAL NEWSPAPERS AND MAGAZINES

AUSTRALIA

Antiques and Collectables for
Pleasure & Profit
PO Box 655
St. Ives, NSW 2075
Australia
+61 – 2-9983-9806
e-mail: info@speediegraphics.com.au

CANADA

Antique Showcase
Trajan Publishing Corp.
PO Box 28103
Lakeport PO
St. Catherines, Ontario
Canada L2N 7P8
905-646-7744
www.trajan.com
e-mail: office@trajan.com or
acseditor@roger.com

Thompsons' Antiques Gazette
418 48th Avenue
PO Box 104
Red Deer, Alberta
Canada T4N 3T2
306-243-4791
e-mail: tgazette@sasktel.net

The Upper Canadian
13 Nelles Blvd.
Grimsby, Ontario
Canada L3M 3P9
905-945-5757
www.theuppercanadian.com
e-mail: sophiebond@theuppercanadian.com

ENGLAND

Antiques Trade Gazette
Circulation Department
115 Shaflesbury Avenue.
London WC2H 8AD
United Kingdom
020 7420 6600
www.atg-online.com
e-mail:
subscriptions@antiquestradegazette.com

Antiques & Art Independent
PO Box 1945
Edinburgh, EH4 1AB
Scotland, United Kingdom
www.antiques-UK.co.UK/independent
e-mail: antiquesnews@hotmail.com

FRANCE

France Antiquitès
Château de Boisriguard
63490 Usson
(04) 73 71 00 04
e-mail: France.Antiquites@wanadoo fr

Le Vie du Collectionneur
b. P. 77
77302 Fontainbleau Cedex
(01) 60 71 55 55

GERMANY

Antiquitäten Zeitung
Nymphenburger Str. 84
D-80636 München
(089) 12-69 90 0

Sammler Journal
Journal-Verlag Schwend GmbH
Schmollerstrasse 31
D-74523 Schwäbisch Hall
(0791 404 500
e-mail: info.sj@t-online.de

Sammler Markt
Der Heisse Draht Verlagsgesellschaft
GmbH & Co.
Drostestr. 14-16
D-30161 Hannover
(0511) 390 91 0
www.dhd24.com

Spielzeug Antik
Verlag Christian Gärtner
Ubierring 4
D-50678 Köln
(0221) 9322266

Tin Toy Magazin
Verlag, Redaktion, Anzeigen, Vertrieb
Mannheimer Str. 5
D-68309 Mannheim
(0621) 739687

Trödler & Sammeln
Gemi Verlags GmbH
Pfaffenhofener Strasse 3
D-85293 Reichertschausen
(08441) 4002 0
www.ag-advertising.de

Index